A Schizophrenic,

TAPPED & SKIPPED

Hope In The Midst Of Madness

J. Mark Stacy

The names and places in this book have been altered to protect the individuals involved. This is an account of almost ten years of my life from my memories. Some scenes have been edited for the sensitivity or benefit of the reader. No malice is intended to any individual or institution. My prayers are with you all.

Reader discretion advised

Scenes in this book may be difficult for some readers to process.

For my children and grandchildren

Dedicated to the people this calling was meant to help.

CONTENTS

Chapter One

TAPPED

As I drove down the road to my daughter's house, my head bobbed back and forth while I navigated slowly through the craters of potholes. These dark, abandoned spaces that encompassed the road reminded me of the run-down lives that dwelled along her street. Lonely houses with ivy and unkept yards where children played with mold-stained toys, situated beside remodeled homes with manicured fenced yards. A perfectly decorated porch with a big "welcome" sign had shades hiding the homeless that slept on the abandoned swing next door. It was despair living next to hope.

Traversing these inescapable dark caverns reminded me of the tumultuous journey that led me here. The potholes, huge and gaping, were unavoidable. No way to go around, to progress a different route. Clinging to God's warring angels, I was plunged into the depths of madness. A hell that played out in a demonic symphony blocked by the hand of God. It was this hand that guided my family and me through this journey. Slowly maneuvering through these potholes in December of 2020, I wandered through the unraveling of events that led me here.

Thunder first woke me on that November night in 2012. I stared at the empty space beside me. My new husband of four years and I had barely been apart. He had taken my young stepchildren, Anna, who was six, and Eric, who was ten, camping for the weekend. They had left on Friday after school to go trout fishing at our favorite spot. The Cumberland River in Kentucky, where my husband and I spent our honeymoon. I would have liked to go, but I was on call at work. Picking up my glasses, I brought my focus to the clock. It read three am.

Another clap of thunder and the phone rang. Even though we'd barely spoken in the last five years, I knew Marissa's voice right away. She was seventeen when I made her leave and live with her dad. A lip piercing broke my tolerance of her constant bidding of my ex-husband against me. Marissa had just gotten her belly button pierced; now, she insisted she needed a stud in her lip. When I told her no, she ran to her dad, who happily took her to poke a large hole that left a scar on her chin. Marissa took full advantage of the non-custodial parent's need to appease. Daily, she reminded me she got along better with him.

For eighteen years, I listened to my ex tell me I wasn't good enough. I wasn't smart enough. "You're stupid if you think you can get that job. You're crazy." He'd told me when I said I was trying to get a steady job with benefits. I got that job, and everything changed. I would go home for lunch at eleven in the morning, and he would still be in bed. Empty rum bottles kept appearing in the trash. He would scream at me for hours when he drank, saying horrible things. The next day he would act as if nothing had happened.

"You're crazy." He'd shout. I heard it over and over.

"Say what you want to me, but if you start treating our kids like this, I'm done," I told him. In 2006, with three beautiful daughters, our marriage was over. Naomi, the oldest, was seventeen. Marissa, the middle, was fifteen. Elyse was eleven. I did my best to navigate the waters of the breakdown of our family.

"Mom, it's like he jumped off a mental cliff." One of my daughters said.

It took almost a year for the divorce to be finalized. I was overwhelmed from dealing with my youngest daughter Elyse's drug addiction. She had turned to drugs to escape the world where her parents were no longer together. I knew Elyse had gotten on the roof when I heard her upstairs window break. She jumped headfirst from the second story in an attempt to end her short life. She was unresponsive to deep pain stimuli all the way to the hospital.

I was distracted by all of that when I decided to make my middle daughter Marissa leave. Since she got along better with her dad, she could live with him. She was strong and determined and good at everything. A dancer and singer and an excellent actress. I didn't realize the gravity of this mistake until later. Regret haunts you when you wish you knew if things would have turned out differently. Something I'd never get the chance to know. Everything I've read about schizophrenia points to the onset being inevitable. But I wish I could have been there to comfort Marissa in those first few scary moments.

Through the phone, I sensed something ominous was happening. "Mom, can I come live with you?" Marissa's voice was uneasy.

Twirling my hair, I walked into the living room, pacing back and forth. I assured Marissa she could come live with me anytime.

"I miss you. How are you doing?" I managed.

"I'm good. Uh thanks, when can you get me?" She seemed relieved.

"Call me tomorrow when you get up." I stammered.

"Oh. Uh, ok." Her voice was shaky.

"Do you need me to get you tonight?" The way she'd hesitated concerned me.

"Uh, no, uh, tomorrow," Marissa said. Click, and she was gone.

Sitting on the couch with my dogs huddled nervously on my lap, I prayed. *Lord, protect her.* Dogs sensed everything, and they all five sat on the sofa with me anxiously waiting to go outside. Opening the sliding door, I breathed in the freshness of the night air.

During the divorce, I heard Marissa was behaving strangely, but I dismissed it as normal teenage behavior under the circumstances. She had called me from a psychiatric facility. Her dad said she was having anxiety issues. Being a drama queen, I thought she was most likely acting out for attention. We'd gone to an amusement park together with a group. She became terrified and got lost. But mostly, we hadn't spent quality time together since I made her leave. I wanted to hug her so badly. I wanted her to know I loved her no matter what.

With my third cup of coffee the following day, I watched the rain pound the windows sideways. Folding the fifth load of laundry, I grew tired of trying to find something on Netflix. After looking at the clock for the thousandth time, I reached for my phone and dialed Marissa.

She answered after four long rings. "Hey, mom, what's up?"

Seriously? I told her about the call at three in the morning, and she acted as if she had no idea what I was talking about.

She said a few words I didn't understand and paused. "Can you come now and pick me up?"

5

"Sure, I'll be there in half an hour." I assured her.

Switching the radio back and forth from the Christian station to the rock station, I wondered what this would be like. My precious middle child Marissa, back in my arms, in my home. I took a moment to be thankful for the chance of improving our strained relationship. Beads of sweat from my hot flash ran into my eyes. Wiping them away, I shifted uneasily in the seat of my car. Five years had gone by, and her voice was so different. *You can do this,* I reassured myself as I turned into the parking lot to pick up this twenty-two-year-old I barely knew.

My gaze darted all around as I texted from the car. "I'm outside in the black Subaru." I wasn't over my Ex's "you're in for the final cut, you are done" message. The protective order was lifted after a year, but being near where he lived was not somewhere I wanted to wait.

Lord, please let her come out quickly. The door opened to a man in a hoodie walking his dog. Behind me, a horn blared, and I jumped.

I texted Marissa again and called multiple times. *Where is she?* Ten miserable minutes later, she emerged from the run-down apartment stairs. She looked different from the daughter I knew. Still the gorgeous, blue-eyed, blond-haired beauty, but there was something underneath.

I couldn't grasp the intuition, but it was like she was Marissa and also something or someone else. She felt different.

Not in the physical sense, but in an otherworldly way. Overwhelming joy and uncomfortableness slapped me in the face. On the ride home, she laughed out loud a couple of times and apologized. Although I thought it was strange, I didn't dwell on it as important.

"Thanks for letting me come. It was, uh, scary there." Marissa exhaled as she settled into the front seat.

I had made up the bed in the room above the garage. It had been my youngest daughter Elyse's room, and it was perfect for a young adult. Marissa thanked me again and plopped down on the bed. Backing off as I leaned in to hug her, I stroked her hair.

"Get some rest. Want grilled cheese?" I offered.

"No, uh, thanks." She looked away as if something distracted her. I just figured she needed time. It was November 3rd, 2012, a key date in my life that I didn't fully understand until later.

My house was two stories with bedrooms connected by an open balcony. My stepdaughter Anna and her friend would perform plays there, treating it like a stage. The bathroom was upstairs along that balcony. At first, I thought Marissa was talking to a friend on the phone. She had the bathroom door open, and her voice echoed through the cathedral ceiling. It was "the laugh." It was distant and higher pitched and best described as disturbing.

"Marissa, is that one of your sisters on the phone?" I asked her, yelling from the couch in the living room.

"No, I don't know where my phone is." She said after too long of a pause. Then her schizophrenic laugh became louder. "Ah, no. I don't know. Yeah, uh-huh, no. I can't." Then she'd laugh.

Suddenly, she emerged after hours of this babbling and shouted. "Can I get a mirror?"

"Of course," I eagerly answered.

"Yeah, I'll get ready." I heard from the hall, and I listened to the click of Marissa's phone this time.

"You have a date?" I teased.

"No, just a friend. Francisco…" She held the "o" for as long as she could and walked out the door.

Alone in the house, I settled in with my dogs. At midnight I was startled by the phone. "Hello?" I answered suddenly wide awake.

"Is this Mrs. Stacy?" A stranger's voice sounded alarmed.

"Do you have a daughter named Marissa?" He asked.

He explained Marissa had banged on their door and told them someone was trying to kill her. He said she told him she had jumped out of her friend's moving car, ran through a neighborhood, and got lost. She said she was terrified and asked me to call her mom.

8

"She is pretty banged up, but she got really upset when I asked if she wanted me to call an ambulance. I'm so glad I got a hold of you." He seemed genuinely concerned. "She wants to talk to you."

"Mom, I'm so scared. Can you come get me, please?" Marissa sounded like a child.

"I'll be right there." I grabbed my keys as the stranger texted me the address.

Her jeans were ripped and wet with the blood from her knee. Her forearms had scrapes over three inches long. Bruises were already visible on the side of her face.

"No, uh, no hospitals," was her response to my pleading and begging to go get her injuries checked.

"We're sorry, we called the police since she said someone was trying to kill her." The strangers looked at me with pity I wasn't yet used to. After thanking them and giving them my address, I helped Marissa stumble to my car. Placing her gently in the front seat, I kissed her matted hair.

"It's going to be ok. I got you." I reassured her, but secretly I was terrified.

On the ride home, I glanced at her sleeping. Her breath, in and out. Tears welled up. I went back to the priceless times I had watched her in her crib. That same soft slumber, that same little nose. I noticed the bruises on her hands from the fall. How could this be happening to my innocent little girl? She felt like my helpless baby when we got home, and I had to half carry her upstairs. Pulling the covers up tightly, I bundled her up. It was our thing to wrap the blanket like a burrito, mommy.

I asked one more time. "Can I please take you for x-rays?" She shook her head and glared at me. "I'll be right back with some Advil and water and Band-aids." She let me put ointment on the scrapes and ice on her bruises. Stroking her hair, I found a new bump and went for another ice pack.

Ding, dong, I opened the door without looking. I knew who it was. "Sorry to bother you at this hour. Does Marissa Mark live here?" The officer asked.

"Yes, but she is finally sleeping," I whispered.

I tried to explain what had happened. "Ah, Marissa was in a friend's car and jumped out because she said the voices told her someone was trying to kill her." This memory of the first police encounter regarding Marissa is etched in my brain.

"Do you feel someone was really trying to kill her?" He asked.

"I don't really know," I replied. "Marissa just came here yesterday, and she said her friend's name was Francesco." The officer didn't insist on waking her. In his face, I saw he had dealt with this behavior before.

Looking me straight in the eyes, he said, "I'm so sorry."

Marissa slept through Sunday and emerged only to grab a box of cereal and a bottle of sweet tea. I bought her new bandages, but she didn't want help, so I left them by her door.

Going to work Monday morning was a relief. I closed my office door that had never been shut. Tears that had been waiting dripped one after another after another. My coworkers knocked softly. My schedule was packed, all four lines on my phone were lit. I kept transferring my calls to another extension. I couldn't talk for several hours.

When I emerged, I opened my mouth to try to explain, and the words just spilled out. "It's Marissa."

One of my coworkers brought me some coffee and the other one a granola bar. They took care of the phones and asked if there was anything they could do. They didn't push me for more information, and the phones were a welcome song.

How could I have explained that she had constantly talked to herself with her schizophrenic laugh for the last two days? My mind drifted back to the weekend and her injuries. Loud knocking on my office door brought me back to my work situation. Overwhelming as my weekend was, I needed to figure out if I could focus or if I needed to take off work. My special HR work line rang.

"Just for today, thanks," I answered, and human resources logged me as unavailable.

At home later that day, I did what I always did. I analyzed the situation. What could I do, how could I help? I was a transportation broker by trade. A person who has made a thirty-year career of being tasked with complex logistical environments, finding solutions, and executing the resolution. In other words, a fixer, a problem solver, a mom.

I was one to go over the top with fixing. When the lawnmower's belt came off, I looked at the schematic and figured out how to put the new one on. When my Ex started his mental cliffhanger, I researched and planned and did everything I could think of to help him. He was my best friend, my husband, the father of our children. Now I was tasked to resolve Marissa's dangerous and terrifying behavior. Surely, there was a fix to this. I researched her symptoms, tried to talk to her about what she was going through. I gently tried to persuade her to go to counselors or to the hospital for treatment. She always glared at me and refused.

Over the next few weeks, her bizarre actions became more and more erratic. She never came out of her room except to smoke. She laughed constantly and uncontrollably until she was exhausted and then slept for days. She would only eat certain things. Chicken breast patties on a specific plate with a circle of ranch dressing with a particular amount of habanero sauce in the middle. Specific kind of stuffed jalapeno peppers with the exact ranch dressing/habanero combo. She would only eat this for a week and smoke in a particular place outside.

Her "voices" were in charge. She was not allowed to bathe, wash her hair, watch tv, or listen to music. All she did was write in her journals. These journals, her writings, were from another place. She wrote about being a white witch. They were written in different directions, as if her brain was sometimes upside down or sideways. They were written as multiple people. They were overwhelming as a mother to read. The "voices" controlled every aspect of her life.

"Marissa?" I tried to get her attention as she swayed back and forth, circling her arms. "Is there anything fun you want to learn or do?"

"I like dancing," was her immediate response.

"What kind of dancing?" I inquired.

"Tap dancing, yeah, I love tapping, tap, tap, tap." She hit her pen on her notebook with the rhythm.

Gently, I persuaded her. "We could get you some tap shoes."

"Yeah, tap shoes, I could go tap, tap, tap," Marissa waved her arms in the air.

Pulling out of the neighborhood, I rolled down my window to escape her scent. At Goodwill, I searched the aisles; I asked the clerk where the dance shoes might be. With luck on our side, I found a pair exactly her size. Fidgeting and uncontrollably talking to the "voices," her arms were again moving in circles around at the orbs.

She said, "they're magic and rule the universe. They control the line." Vivid hallucinations had become her added and constant companion.

Yes, people stared at us. She hadn't bathed for a week or more and had worn the same clothes. It was a project to get her in the car, let alone go somewhere. I paid as quickly as possible. A few people allowed me to get in front of them. They just wanted us out of there. She had gone ahead of me, and I fumbled with the keys, quickly unlocking the car. Falling into the driver's seat, I got the keys in the ignition.

Caught by the air that had escaped the car, I paused. A disturbing silence was present, chills went up my back, and I felt the hair rise to the top of my head. Inhaling, I froze in my seat. Evil, I felt it all around me with penetrating darkness. With the red eyes of a stranger, that evil existence looked me up and down. Death staring at me, my schizophrenic Marissa started screaming uncontrollably. Wild catlike, screeching.

The terror in her eyes told of her inability to stop. She went on and on. "You don't understand. You can't go. No, I'm in charge. I'm in charge of the line. I, I, I'm the white witch. I control the line." On and on about Magicland and white witch and that she ruled over it. For two and a half hours, I sat there, unable to move. Trapped in the parking lot of Goodwill. The

14

bag with the tap shoes was still on my lap as I sat behind that wheel.

Because she was so loud, a few people motioned to me as if to ask if I needed help. All I could do was nod for them to move on. She finally lost her voice and became silent. Utter sadness came to the car. She began to sob.

As the tears streamed down, she whispered hoarsely, "I'm so sorry, mom."

Her head was down now, and she couldn't be consoled. I felt my precious child crying out. I just cried with her for about an hour. We had made it to the intersection by my house. I had to pull over, and we just sat there, neither able to speak.

I finally said, "I can try to understand. It will be ok." A lie. I had no idea. As I pulled into my driveway, I searched for something to say. With bloodshot eyes, I could only ache for her. "I love you no matter what. I'll do what I can to help."

"I'm gonna lay down now." She said, implying she didn't want me to go with her.

Standing at her door, I heard her whimpering. *Lord, please help me find a way to help her.* I prayed and lingered there until she was silent.

The following day before I left for work, I quietly knocked and left the tap shoes just inside her door. I somehow had to manage a very stressful job, a household, wonderful children, stepchildren, my loving husband, and five dogs. All four lines constantly rang as my hectic workday was a necessary element to the stack that sat in the wooden "bills to pay" box.

Focusing was not happening, as my thoughts ever lingered back to that parking lot. My thirty years of experience meant I could basically fly blindly through every detail of my workday. "Covered the Walmart load to Scranton." I yelled from my desk, "Got that Custom load to New Jersey." Thank you, Lord, for this easy workday. I praised God as I got in my car.

What were you thinking? My mother's guilt hit me as I made my way down the hill to my exit. Mindless through traffic, I chastised myself. *Why would you take her out when she clearly wasn't ready?*

When I raised the garage door after the long day, I saw some marks on the floor and tiny drops that appeared to be blood. Blood in little drops with slide marks making them look like a T. Rushing into the house, my eyes darted and glanced all around. Sitting at the kitchen table, my husband was startled as I burst into the room.

"Where is Marissa?" I demanded as he looked puzzled at me.

"I think she's in her room, there was a thump earlier, but I didn't go check on her." I heard as I ran up the stairs.

Taking a deep breath, I paused. I didn't want to appear as panicked as I was. As softly as possible, I knocked on my daughter's door.

Her voice still hoarse from screaming, she managed a whisper, "Yeah?"

It was the best yeah I had ever heard. I breathed for the first time since arriving and asked her about her day and if she was feeling better. I hesitated... *What do you say when you are in this situation?* I struggled to keep from running in and hugging her as tightly as possible. Of course, I thought she was lying there bleeding to death.

She then pointed at the tap shoes that were covered in blood. "I practiced all day, but they told me to stop." She pointed both index fingers on either side of her temples. Her feet were covered up on the bed, so I couldn't see them. By the amount of blood, I knew they would still be bleeding.

"I, I, love tapping, yeah." She tapped on her notepad with her pen again.

"I noticed some blood?" I asked.

"Yeah, I couldn't stop, but it's cool."

"I'll be back with some Band-aids. Need anything?" I spouted.

"I'm good." She waved me away.

She continued to tap dance in the garage all day for a couple of weeks. She reveled at being able to do such a joyful thing. Once I was home when she was tapping, I heard her perform an entire play. I wanted to watch, but I didn't want to interrupt such a rare moment of her happily reenacting something she had enjoyed in her youth. I cleaned up the blood daily before bringing her new bandages to her room each night.

One evening she emerged from her room, took a shower, and said, "I want to take tap dance lessons so I can get better." It worked. She just needed a hobby, something to bring her mind into focus. I found a school that offered adult classes the next day and signed her up for a trial.

She was childlike, getting ready and worrying about what to wear, and wanted pink tights. What takes blood out of leather? I searched the internet for ideas. I got her tap shoes as clean as possible, and we headed to the class. She was so beautiful; her hair was clean and shiny. She had curled it and put it in a big ponytail. A pink ribbon wrapped around the holder. Taking my hand, she twirled around and curtsied and bowed. I felt that little girl's giddiness in my Marissa in that remarkable moment.

Sitting in the lobby nervously, I listened for any schizophrenic laughter or her talking to the "voices." Reveling in the achievement of just being a mom with a girl in tap class, I looked around at the other parents. A toddler played with toys as his mommy searched her purse for his binky. A dad talked on the phone in his clear, stern, work voice. I was so happy to have found something Marissa loved.

Not trusting the normalness, my ears tried to catch every tap, every voice, every single sound. After half an hour, Marissa abruptly stumbled from behind the curtain and ran outside. The sparkle was gone, and her face was distorted. I ran after her, and she stopped at the edge of the parking lot. She was uncontrollably shaking, sweating, and her feet were bleeding.

"What happened? Can I help?" I frantically tried to console her.

She stared up and started talking to the "voices" and laughing and demanded: "Just take me to my room."

This was an arrogant voice, a different voice than the one that had been there a second ago. Shocked by the rapid change, I stepped back. Marissa's character had changed. A different persona had taken charge. Her face was contorted, and her eyes dull to the world. Her chin dipped down as if she was looking down at me. Shocked and overwhelmed, I paused. I had no idea what to do.

Trying to console this new persona, I held out the coat. Marissa wasn't there. This new persona snatched it from my hands and flung it over her shoulder. She threw herself toward me and pulled back again. Hesitantly, I turned to go back to the car. She followed me plopping into the seat like she owned the world.

When I turned the key, the radio blared. "Turn that off!" This new persona demanded. Startled by the quick movement, I once again froze.

"You don't get to go." She started screaming in a high-pitched, harrowing, penetrating tone. Her "character" took over. It was a much different scream than before. This was another person's scream. No one would have known the difference except me. I prayed, *God, help my daughter, please help my daughter.* I had no way to get away and no clue what to do.

She screamed, "you know that I am magic and that I'm a white witch and I'm the queen and I'm in charge, I'm magic! I live in the line, the line that is everywhere. You just don't get it." The line… This was a common theme. As I tried to breathe, she screamed and screamed and screamed. "Why did you bring me here, Mom? You know I'm in charge of the witches!" I tried not to notice the terror in her eyes, the sad confusion. Finally, she lost her voice, started sobbing, and my sweet precious Marissa came back.

As I started the car, she leaned her head on my shoulder. Sniffling, she whispered. "I, I'm so sad, mom, so sad, I don't know what to do, mom, I'm so sad."

I smoothed her face and searched for what to say. "I'm so sorry. I love you so much." We sat there with the car running until the parking lot was empty. "Let's get you home. It'll be ok." I attempted to reassure her.

"I'm just so sad, mom." She whimpered through her tears.

"I'm so sorry," I muttered as I tried to focus on the road. Sadness and fear gripped me. I had no idea how to help her.

She never touched her tap shoes again. I found them later buried in a box in her closet with shredded paper and old bloody socks. I threw them out, shuddering at the memory of the two of us just sitting in that parking lot. I never imagined these first heartbreaking episodes, through November and December 2012, were only the beginning of our journey.

Chapter Two

THE DIAGRAM

I have wandered many roads in my lifetime. Driving was my therapy when I was upset or confused or, in this case, utterly defeated, overwhelmed, and devastated. Mindless wandering freed me of burden, just me and the road. So with a full schedule on my work plate, dinner planning, baseball schedules, and all things stepmom, wife, and household, I took off meandering through the streets. With the windows down for a moment, the brisk air was supposed to renew my soul. Caught by the chill that reminded me of those episodes, I quickly rolled them back up.

I couldn't find my way through this illness that had taken over my daughter. The word "schizophrenic" kept playing like a bad dream, a nightmare with no end. My precious child Marissa was gone. No one except those who have dealt with having mentally ill children could understand the devastating loss.

There was no fixing this. I had to find a way to accept this new version of her. My love never stopped regardless. But this wasn't my sweet innocent little freckled-faced baby. I hadn't been able to find a solution, no route, no way through this madness. I just drove aimlessly while my thoughts drifted to my innocent little girl.

Marissa was a blue-eyed, blond-haired, freckle-faced little spitfire. Her older sister Naomi was an accomplished gymnast from a young age, and Marissa wanted to be just like her. She had this little plaid leotard that she'd had for a year. It was too big, but Marissa wore it anyway. One day she came running over to me and proudly pranced in front of the mirror with the leotard on. It was the cutest thing ever. "Look, mommy, I grew into this body."

She was not afraid of anything. Her sister Elyse was an All-Star softball player. One evening during softball season, the commentator wanted someone to sing the National Anthem. Marissa and a friend volunteered. Her friend chickened out, but not Marissa. O'er the land of the freeeeeeeeeee, e, and the homeeeeeee of the brave, she brilliantly belted out a perfect rendition. That was Marissa.

Her older sister, Naomi, had a hard time with back tucks. Marissa did it the first time she tried. She was determined and relentless, a talented actress, and even decided to become a welder. Marissa was at the top of her class in Mig welding. She wanted to go into the Navy and do underwater welding. Her severe heart murmur kept her from passing the fitness test. How could this be happening? What can I do? A million unanswered questions. I drove around, trying to navigate my thoughts. I felt loss, incredible loss... I missed my daughter, and I wanted her back. I fought back the tears that would make the drive unsafe.

My youngest daughter Elyse, who had the addiction issue, was doing a little better. Since she had been to every counselor in the area, I wanted her input on who had helped her.

Dialing her from my car, she answered right away. "Hey, mom, is everything ok?"

"Yeah, I wanted to see if you could tell me which counselor you found most helpful." I wrestled with words that wouldn't offend her.

Elyse immediately replied, "Lisa, she is the only one that really listened. Thanks for asking me." Elyse seemed thrilled I had asked.

I pulled in my drive as I waved to the neighbor. Grateful to be able to talk with my youngest daughter.

The next day I reached out to Lisa's office. "I'm their mom. We met when Elyse had her assessment. Marissa is her sister." I prayed the voicemail was monitored regularly.

Within a few minutes, Lisa called back. I knew this counselor heard all of the divorce/family stories from Elyse. The "assessment" for troubled teens occurred after Elyse was kicked out of school for the third time.

"I'd be glad to talk with her." Lisa recognized the urgency in my voice.

"I can't shake the feeling something is changing, and I don't know what to do." I tried to explain. Lisa paused, and I heard papers shuffling.

"Try to get her in here as soon as possible." We arranged around five the next day, March 13, 2013.

Cautiously, I listened at Marissa's door. No laughing or talking so far. "Marissa, it's mom. Can I come in?" I softly knocked on the door. "I brought you a bowl of peanut butter Captain Crunch" (her favorite). "I bought food for Charles Bob." I had gotten her a cat to keep her company. I did not join her in the fondness of cats.

"Charles Bob, yeah, Charles Bob, I shall call you." She said as she tapped the cat on the head.

"You have to feed him and change his litter box," I told her.

"Yeah, ok, yeah, uh, ok." I must have been desperate if I was willingly cleaning out a litter box for a cat. I knew she wouldn't do it.

Knocking again, this time a little louder, then finally, I heard a faint "yeah." I moved very slowly as I wasn't sure what this week's triggers were. I sat the cereal and cat food down. I asked if I could move the filthy clothes to the other pile so I could sit in the chair, but she didn't look up. She apathetically said, thanks, mom, and started devouring the cereal like she hadn't eaten in days. I sat down on top of an old pizza box, and I gathered my nerves.

"Would you like to try to get the voices to stop?" I asked softly.

Her body froze. I inhaled and held my breath. An eerie silence engulfed the room—as if terror met hope and pure desperation. Tears welled up in her eyes, and for a very brief moment, I saw her, my sweet Marissa, without the veil of schizophrenia.

With a whimper, she managed, "I'd like to try."

"I asked Elyse what counselor helped her." Marissa's eyes twinkled at the mention that another member of our family was trying to help. "Her name is Lisa, and she could see you tomorrow. I'll stay right with you," I reassured. "Want to get cheeseburgers on the way?" I tried to make it as normal as I could. Marissa looked stunned and just managed to nod.

The next hectic workday went way too slow. I found myself looking at the time on my computer nearly constantly. I wanted to take off, but I was in charge of too many projects, and I was blessed (and cursed) to be the breadwinner. Everyone counted on me. I rushed out the door, and my car drove itself home.

Knocking softly, "Marissa?" I prayed she remembered our conversation and her willingness to get help.

"I'm ready." she pulled open the door, and Charles Bob rushed out. The dogs started barking and chased him under the couch.

"You can wait on the porch; I'll be right there." I motioned to Marissa as my stepson helped me wrangle Charles Bob back to her room. I took a long glance at the chaos all around her existence. The smell of cat urine, days-old food cartons, old cigarettes that she had hidden in her dresser drawer. *Lord, please help me know how to reach her.* I prayed as I quickly shut the door. She was waiting on the porch with her hands swirling around, and her eyes wouldn't focus and were moving in circles, following an invisible object.

The car ride was oddly silent. "Did you want a cheeseburger?" I shakily asked. Her eyes were moving up and down with her hands that were jerking and arching. Her wrists twisted back and forth with a few of her notorious schizophrenic laughs. She didn't acknowledge my question. Turning into Wendy's, I could tell she was happy by the exciting shift in her stance.

"Single, cheese, and ketchup only, please," I yelled into the speaker. Marisa grabbed the cheeseburger as if it was the first one she had ever tried. Gulping it down with the water I had in the cupholder. I realized she probably hadn't eaten since the bowl of cereal.

Lisa's office was empty as it was past working hours. "No, I don't want you to come," Marissa pointed at me.

Five minutes later, Lisa came and got me. "She doesn't know why she's here," Lisa puzzled.

I sat in the cozy chair that reminded me of all the other counselor's cushy chairs I had sat in before.

I looked at my sweet child. "Tell her about when you died. Tell her about the line. Tell her about Magicland." Marissa's eyebrows went up, showing the "oh yeah," like she figured out what to talk about. "Tell her about the dead people constantly trying to get you to fix their problems." I reminded her. Marissa started rambling on and on.

"Are you seeing things right now?" Lisa tried following Marissa's eyes which were darting around and her hands followed just like she had her hand out the car window.

Marissa explained the orbs and angels and tried to explain the line. "It's all the time like it never stops day and night and day and night." Marissa tightened her body.

Sensing her inability to stop, Lisa said, "I'm so sorry. I can't imagine how difficult that must be. It must be so hard not being able to turn them off." She showed my sweet little girl genuine empathy for the illness that plagued her mind. "Marissa, do you want them to go away?" Lisa asked.

Marissa paused and tried to focus past the orbs and "voices." "I want to get better. I want to be normal." A sadness immediately engulfed the room. The air temperature seemed to drop ten degrees, and I shivered at the triggers flying all around.

As Lisa got on the phone with the mental hospital, I felt hope for the first time. "It's going to be ok; I'm so proud of you," I said as I wrapped my sweater around Marissa's shoulders and squeezed her. The tap-dancing incident played in my head, the months of struggle she had endured. *Lord, please help my precious child.*

The ride home to get her a few things and the next ride to the hospital were extremely terrifying—for both of us. She had a few outbursts, and some of her talking was disturbing and in different "voices." She continued to move her eyes and her arms at the circling orbs. I could feel her shifting in and out.

"May I help you?" the receptionist said as she slid open the glass divider.

"We have an intake appointment for Marissa Mark." We checked into the front waiting lobby. "Marissa, they said sit over here." I directed her.

"Please, babe, please stay." I heard a husband beg his wife as she ran out the double doors. A tweaker's mother stood over him, holding his baby, reminding him why he needed to get clean. Parents sitting with the "I don't want to live" teen. The disparaged hopelessness showed in the wrinkles on all of their faces.

It seemed to take a year to get to the interior intake waiting area. This is an entirely separate area behind the locked double doors and the metal detectors. Beige walls with psychotic ink scribbles, the smell of disinfectant mixed with nervous body odor. Old moldy carpet and fluorescent lighting. The faces of despair wrapped in fear with sides of utter sadness and hopelessness were all seated there. I thought how ironic it was that Marissa's beauty still shined through in this desolate place.

She sat struggling and mumbling and uncontrollably circling her arms. "It'll be ok. Hang in there." I kept reassuring her as I watched her face twitching and her brow wrenching. Four long hours later, they called her name.

"We're going to room one." The interviewer pointed to the number over the door of the cramped little room. "Can you spell your name?" She asked Marissa, who struggled to answer any of the questions. Required forms, one after another. Question after question, one after another after another. When the documents were done, she left us alone in the room. I couldn't help but stare at the clock. Marissa had gone silent, and she was twitching.

"Hang in there. You're doing great. I'm so very proud of you." My mind was blank, trying to find anything positive to add to this horrifying situation.

After another hour, the interviewer's keys abruptly rattled on the door. We both jumped. "Ok, they're going to admit her."

Turning, I reassured her. "Marissa, they're going to take you to your room. I'm so proud of you. I love you no matter what." I leaned to her attempting to hug her, but she shrugged away. There was no feeling of my precious child. Dull, lifeless, and unable to focus on anything, she couldn't control her eye movements or hug me back.

When the door alarm slammed, and she was safely inside the hospital area, my knees surrendered to the weight. The nurse caught my arm. "You ok?"

"Yeah, sorry, I just forgot to eat, and we've been here five hours." I steadied myself.

"I'm so sorry. There were a lot of people that checked in at the same time. Full moon, I guess. I have some crackers in the office." She offered.

"I'm ok," I muttered as I lost grip of the weight of the door, and it crashed behind me.

They led me out the second set of alarm blaring doors. Their utter pity made me even more nauseous. Once in the car, the tears came. *Thank you, Lord, please help my little girl.* Relief and sadness slammed into me like a wreck. *She will get the help she needs.*

I repeated to myself as streams of tears dripped one by one. I need to get home. I forced reality to the surface.

"They're keeping her." I texted my husband.

"Are you ok to drive?"

"Yeah, I just need a minute." I whimpered. He knew that was code for, no, I'm not ok. My daughter is crazy, and I don't know how to help her.

"Are you sure you should drive? I can come and get you?"

"I'll be fine. Need me to pick up anything? I'm stopping for some beer." He knew I was going to need those to sleep.

Walking in the door, cracking open my beer, I decided I needed to see Marissa's room for some kind of closure. Reassurance that a hospital behind closed doors with strangers was necessary for her to get help. Upstairs, a long hall connected the main house to her room over the garage. There was a trail of coffee spills. Candles couldn't cover the intense odor of old food containers, piles of clothes she'd worn for weeks and wouldn't allow me to touch. All mixed with the rankness of cat urine. I wondered if homeless people smelled like these clothes. I went about trying to gather the remnants of her existence in this space. This was my chance to clean her clothes and bed linens. Her response was always. No, uh, thanks. I was oddly excited to make this place clean.

The notebook was covered up on her bed with a torn sheet. A red marker had bled onto the covers in a large circle. I had to read it. I needed to see it. Trembling at the words, I read each one. At the top of the page, she had scribbled, My Death Diagram. Mother's intuition had known of this hell on earth. There, on those pages, lay a well-planned, detailed diagram—my daughter's death plan.

Pictures illustrated the torn sheets knotted together, her looping them and fastening them around her neck. How she would secure them to the solid wood on her bed frame. The Plan told of her climbing on the rooftop out her second-floor window and jumping. She had a detailed sketch of herself lifeless, hanging by the torn, knotted sheets. Then I noted the date. March 12, she had planned to do this the night I came to her room. The night I had asked her, "would you like to try to get the voices to stop?"

Chapter Three

MEDICATIONS

Shivering, I drove myself to the hospital, clasping the wheel tightly. It had been another exhausting, fix-all my problems day. I had been screamed at a lot for not getting a shipment delivered on time. Like I had driven the truck, controlled the weather, and people who had accidents. Sometimes customers yelled at me because they could. I was not ready to see my daughter in this place. It's not like there's a class, preparation for visitation with a schizophrenic daughter, 101. Driving around twice, I found a spot in the third row from the back. All with the same grieving despair behind their fake smiles, parents and loved ones filed in. Some with bags of clothing or toiletries to check-in. *Everything is going to be ok. She will be ok.*

I parked and reread the rules. No strings, no zippers, no sharp objects, no plastic bags, no looped items. Then on to visitation rules. No cell phones, no keys, no purses, no wallets, nothing in pockets. Everything has to be left in your car, or a small locker can be assigned to you ahead of time. The check-in process for visitation was longer than the actual visitation.

Disinfectant lingered in the air. A loud blaring alarm sounded as the doors opened to that space. Like kindergarteners, we were asked to line up in a single file and be respectful and quiet. Twitching and scratching, I noticed the familiar signs of the withdrawing addict to my right. I could smell the stale cigarettes and whiskey covered by tic tac on a couple there to see their son. As I sat in my assigned kindergartener chair in the cafeteria of this place, Marissa's face as a little girl crept in. Her freckles and sparkling blue eyes with youth's wonder and innocence. I listened to the lady softly whisper, asking if Kleenex was ok to bring in.

Abruptly and with that same loud alarm, the door opened, and the patients shuffled in a single file. Some of the loved ones cried out to them and embraced. At first, I didn't recognize Marissa. She had her head down, and her hair covered her face. She slowly, reluctantly, came to my side and sat down when she saw me.

"Why did you bring me here, mom?" She suddenly screamed.

Shocked and startled, I couldn't move, and security came over to our table. I took a breath and managed. "You said you wanted to get better." Marissa started sobbing. The guard relaxed as she melted into my shoulder.

Her tears moistened my sleeve. "It's so embarrassing, mom, all the stuff I did and said. It's too hard. I want to go back. Why did you bring me here?" Her voice elevated. "I don't want to get better anymore!" She was happier, not knowing she was sick. "I don't want help. Take me home, mom," she sobbed. "Please, take me home where I'm safe." Sadness filled her eyes. "Mom, is there any way the dead people are really trying to get me to solve their problems?" She looked at me, desperate for reality to be hers.

"I'm sorry." My tears started to flow.

"Please, mom, I can't stay here anymore. They want me to take more medicine tomorrow. I will not!" She screamed. The chilling, unsettling voice I'd heard before—a different voice than the pleading. An hour can be a very long time. I tried not to glance at the clock. "Please take me out of this place. Please, mom, I want to feel safe. I'm scared, mom, please." Relentlessly, she begged over and over.

"Can we get you some water?" A concerned staff member offered.

"No, thanks," I muttered as I saw the look of pity. The same look from the Goodwill parking lot and the parents at the dance school. Concern mixed with gratitude that they weren't in my shoes.

Hugging her shell, I held her too long, and she pulled away. "I'm so proud of you. You are so brave. I know you can do this. Please let them help you get better." I couldn't imagine having a mind that played such tricks on me. How hard that would be to realize the things you'd done and said made you look insane. "I love you no matter what; please give it a couple more days." Without looking back, she shuffled back in line, waiting for the few patients whose loved ones lingered. With the loud buzz of the door, we lined up single file and escaped that horrible scene.

In the car, I wrestled with what I had said. Did I do the right thing? Did I say the right things? What else could I have done? I couldn't go back, but I had this conversation in my head over and over. There isn't a rule book for what to say to a schizophrenic daughter while she realizes her illness. At least not one that I'd found. Much was written about the illness itself, but what was most personally difficult was her realizing that her actions made her appear crazy. Utter sadness filled her eyes. Her torment of knowing how she had acted and talked to things that weren't real. The eyes of my broken-hearted, devastated, horrified, and terrified daughter.

Pulling out of the parking lot, I prayed, *Lord, please protect her and watch over her.* "I'm on my way home. Need anything?" I called my husband from the car.

"No, I'm good. How was Marissa?" He asked.

"Not good. I'm stopping to pick up beer. Love you."

Feverishly, I tried to find a support group for Marissa. I found a lot of support groups for the caregiver. But I wanted a group she could connect with. Friends that could relate to her unique view of the world. I tried to find functioning schizophrenics that could connect with her. I would understand in the months to come, but at the time, she would be well in my naive fixer mind. I read every paper from the mental hospital, called every support number. They all said the same thing. She has to want to get help. She has to want to come to our sessions.

Tapping on the steering wheel and fidgeting in my seat, I pulled into the pick-up patient area. I took in a long, slow inhale. Just breathe; she'll be ok. I had talked with her a couple of days after the visitation, and her voice was completely different.

"I'm trying to get better; I want to be normal." She had been in the mental hospital for fifteen days.

Her doctor stressed over and over. "She has to take the medication exactly as prescribed."

I was tasked with four different pills and a shot once a month.

"Marissa will get a loading dose of the shot just before she's released." He added. With the discharge plan arranged and the papers signed, it was just a waiting game. My leg bounced, and I was twirling my hair. I watched and listened for the familiar buzz of the door. Waiting for a mental patient to be released was a clockmaker's nightmare. Tick, tick, tick. Ever wondering, would it be a time bomb or a bath bomb?

With the door blare, I caught sight of Marissa's brown hair. The smell of cheap shampoo lingered, and I figured they'd made her bathe before releasing her. I secretly hoped she had wanted to be clean and that things would be different in that regard. Smiling as she saw me, I couldn't contain my utter relief to see her. I ran to her and hugged her tightly. She hugged me back. Gripping me tightly like a daughter hugs a mother she has missed.

"Can we go now?' Marissa was anxious as we signed the last papers and gathered her belongings.

Holding the door for a moment, the fear and the memory of the evil voice caught me off guard. *No, God's got this.* I reminded myself.

My husband had taken his kids fishing for the weekend again. This was a good time for my young stepchildren to be away. Breathing a sigh of relief, I watched Marissa's sweet slumber as we made our way home. Words didn't come easy to the question: What do you say to a child that just got released from a mental hospital? How was your stay? They had given her the loading dose of a medication. I assumed that was the reason for her immediate slumber.

"Marissa, we're home." Waking her as I pulled in the drive.

"Uh, ok, thanks." She mumbled.

"Can you walk?" I asked.

"Yeah, I think so." We barely got up the stairs together.

"We'll go over the new rules later," I said, noticing her glazed-over look.

I had gotten her a happy, peaceful, brightly colored comforter and new sheets. Her room had been thoroughly disinfected. All the clothes that could be salvaged were washed and put away. Her dresser had been wiped clean of the filth of a thousand burned-out cigarettes. The torn sheets were destroyed. A new journal and her favorite gel pens were lying in a neat pile. A fresh start.

Pulling the covers up tightly, she marveled. "Thanks, mom. So soft and cozy." She ran her blue-painted chipped nails, smoothing the comforter. Her freckled cheeks were pale from the lack of sunlight. Like a little girl giggling, she reached for her new pajamas. "Can I put these on?" Marissa excitedly picked up the pj's like they were treasures.

"Sure," I said like it was Christmas morning. "Want grilled cheese and tomato soup?" We smiled as we both knew those were comfort foods that she loved.

Things were going to be normal, right? I thanked God for that moment. The smell of grilled cheese and tomato soup reminded me of great times with my family. After long weekends camping, my mother would always serve us this meal. Happy memories of my youth. So many emotions were brought to the surface. Comfort and peace and joy and the innocence of a child. I wanted Marissa to have those feelings.

The following day, I was anxious to welcome this new version of Marissa. Cinnamon and vanilla raised our home to another level. Now that I was the mom, I wondered what emotions were evoked by the smell of my special pancakes. I was anxious to have my sweet girl awake to a new day. *Please Lord, let her be ok.* Constantly, I prayed and prayed for her to have relief from the torment of her own mind.

It was Saturday, and I hesitated to make any plans. I knew at any moment, Marisa would be waking. I drank coffee and dreamed of a time when she was innocent of the horrors life could bring. I tried not to cry over the loss of that innocence and be thankful for the peace of that moment. I drank my black coffee in the silence of my suburban backyard—the pancakes, now cold and tucked in the microwave. My five dogs romped about in our privacy-fenced existence. I binge-watched That 70's Show. I laundered every bedsheet that wasn't being slept on— dusted every shelf and picture. But she didn't wake up. I was determined not to wake her. Stubbornness, it runs in my family, and I am no exception.

At four pm, I couldn't take Ashton Kutcher anymore. I coasted myself upstairs to Marissa's room with two beers in, angry at waiting. Very softly, I knocked. No answer. A little louder, I knocked. Nothing. A lot louder, I knocked. My mind drifted to the diagrams laid out on her bed when I tried the door. The red marker "blood" stains on her sheet. Do not panic, do not panic. Why was my sweet child so silent? Without breathing, I crept slowly to her bedside.

"Marissa? Hey, are you ok? It's getting late." Do not panic, do not panic. My heart started racing.

"Huh? Mom?" She wiped sleepish wonder from her eyes. My heart leaped from my throat.

Since I'd been staring at the space for hours, I decided I wanted some candles and new knick-knacks for the living room shelves. "Do you want to go to Hobby Lobby with me?" *Holy crap. Is that all I can think of to do that is normal?* I thought.

Sheepishly she said, "Sure."

"Ok, I'm ready when you are," I said as I closed her door and made my way to the kitchen for a cup of coffee.

Maybe doing something normal after being in a mental hospital would be a welcome change. I allowed myself to be excited that Marissa wanted to come. She emerged from her room and went into the dark bathroom. I heard the swish of the sweater and the zipper on her pants. The familiar teeter while trying to put on shoes while standing on one leg. Real shoes. You don't need shoes when you aren't going outside. I wondered if she had missed the feeling.

Slowly, she navigated the stairs. "I'm ready."

The silence was interrupted only by whizzing cars as we made our way. Her sleepy blue eyes twinkled with delight as she took in the world. Sun beamed on her face, and she soaked the rays like she'd been in a cave for years, and this was the first time she had witnessed the sunshine. I drove slowly so she could see everything she seemed to be relishing. At the Hobby Lobby, her head darted around.

I had a clock and a vanilla-scented candle in my cart. When I looked up, I noticed Marisa's mouth! It was Wide open! Not like, "oh my," but completely wide open. Tears were running down her face.

"Mom, I can't control my mouth. I think something is wrong." She struggled to say with her mouth gaping open.

Shocked, I jerked sideways and lost grip of a small decanter, and it clanged on the floor. Immediately, I saw panic in my sweet child's face as the entire store seemed focused on her.

"It's gonna be ok; it's going to be ok," I reassured her. Quickly, I left my cart and put my arm around her. Cautiously, we made it to the car.

"Mom, I can't close my mouth."

"Please, Marissa, let me take you to the hospital," I begged.

"Mom, I just got out of the hospital. Please don't take me back." I could barely make out, but the panic in her eyes at that thought made me drive home as fast as I could. Wrapping her in a blanket from my emergency car stash, I slowly walked her up the stairs. "I'm just tired. I'm gonna sleep. Uh, I think it's getting better." She tried to say.

Sitting on the bed, watching her mouth gaping open while she drifted off, I prayed. *Lord, please let her be ok.* After an hour or so, she seemed to sleep peacefully.

In another hour, I tiptoed to her side. Her mouth was still open, but she looked peaceful. I decided to go get groceries. This was the universal mother thing. Fix things with food. For forty minutes, I picked out the normalcy of my life at the grocery.

Then my phone rang. It was Marissa. "Mom, where are you? I need you to take me to the hospital? I can't close my mouth, and it's my tongue."

I couldn't understand all the words. Hospital, tongue, panic! I broke every speed limit and ran all the lights. She was on the balcony, just standing there. Her tongue was pointed and hanging out of her mouth. It was otherworldly.

I panicked. "It'll be ok, it'll be ok, it'll be ok," I repeated too many times. *What the hell!?* Without unpacking the groceries, I put the same blanket over her shoulders. "Let's get you in the car. It's going to be ok." *Yeah, right! My daughter's tongue is pointed straight out of her mouth that she can't close!* I tried to breathe, inhale, exhale, breathe. Don't panic. Too late... Ok... Drive to the hospital... Don't wreck. Don't wreck. Don't wreck.

Dystonic reaction, I had never heard of this. What the hell was that? The ER a**hole was not sympathetic to our situation. You could tell he had dealt with this reaction before. He could go to hell. Or maybe have lived ours for a day. An allergic reaction to an antipsychotic makes a person's body distort. The "loading dose" of the Invega Sustenna caused my sweet daughter Marissa to have an allergic reaction. After a few tests and a few hours, they gave her anti-reactive medications.

I called my parents, and they came to the hospital. My dad drove my groceries still in the trunk to my house, and my mom tried to console Marissa. I would never forget the look on my mom's face. Who wanted to see their grandchild with her tongue pointed out, unable to control her muscles? Marissa kept thanking me for taking her to the hospital. She was in so much pain. After being released twice the same weekend from a hospital, she fell into her bed and slept.

The next day, I checked on her over and over. I couldn't stop worrying. I called into work and searched for the words to explain the situation. I typed: "My child was released from the mental hospital only to have to go to the emergency room the same day because her tongue was pointed and she couldn't close her mouth." There, that should do it. "I need to watch her and check for side effects for the next couple of days."

For three long days, she slept. The doctor from the mental hospital called me and apologized. I had called and left him a message as I panicked on my way to the ER that night. "I'm so sorry," he repeated multiple times. He knew dystonic reactions were so painful. He was genuinely regretful. Later my opinion would change, but at this time, I thought he was genial for personally calling.

Marissa was so confused and scared. "Did you want to go for a walk?" She didn't seem to know what I meant. "Can I bring you ice cream?" I searched for anything that would bring her joy. For another two weeks, she went everywhere I went. She went to work with me and just sat next to me all day. She was afraid. Afraid of the world. Fearful of the reality that was slowly creeping in. The medicine was starting to work.

Day after day, she became more aware of her illness. No one understands that this was the difficult part. When they realized they were ill. When they get depressed from the realization. When they didn't want to know. Embarrassed by the previous actions, they started to remember. This was the sadness. To have been naive was golden.

Reality smacked them with zero friends. The ones they once had were afraid of their illness or of them for some behavior they had no control of. The "voices" and images that were so familiar were gone. They're left feeling so alone. A loneliness that only another schizophrenic would understand.

Their world was gone. Schizophrenics' normal was hearing and seeing things that aren't there twenty-four hours a day, seven days a week. Society's normal was so quiet—Like an isolation chamber. The suicide rate haunted me. Of one hundred schizophrenics, ten of them kill themselves. Reality sucked. My daughter deserved to live a better life than this. This was a disease of the brain. Surely there was a cure. She was going to be ok, right?

She had to get this shot every month, or her symptoms would return. The doctor assured me that the loading dose caused the reaction and that a standard amount would be ok. I made all the appointments on the discharge papers. She was still on her father's insurance, and I was so thankful. The monthly shot was three thousand dollars without coverage. That didn't include the prescribed sleep medication and antidepressants. Over and over, they stressed the importance of the shot. "If she ever goes off the shot, her mind will decompress, and she may never be able to be this well again." It was repeated multiple times.

I picked up her meds and watched her take them and paid the fifty-dollar copay per prescription. There never seemed to be anything about recovery in all the appointments and information I read. Nothing took all her symptoms away. She continued to hear bearable, non-dark "voices." She continued to see things that weren't there. I could only find information about the management of symptoms.

My life took a backseat. Months went by, and I somehow had to learn to celebrate the good through the pain. My wonderful husband, my two other beautiful daughters, my young stepchildren, my close extended family, my five dogs, my stressful job… Breathe… just breathe. One day at a time… I told myself. *God, where do I go from here?*

Chapter Four

DISABLED?

Little burnt pieces of foil. What the hell are those? Balled up burnt pieces of foil in my daughter Marissa's dresser drawer? When it comes to education about illegal substances. I would have gotten an F in the subject. Since my youngest Elyse was an addict for so long, you would think I'd know more about what that stuff looked like. She was addicted to pills. This was some weird stuff. Saving Elyse was my focus, not trying to understand the way anything looked.

When I first worked at my meaningless job, I had a roach clip to hang up my kid's pictures. You know, one of those clip-looking things that I found out holds marijuana cigarettes. I had no idea what it was. It had pretty feathers on it. Being Native American, I was attracted to things with feathers. I had even gotten a tattoo with a feather. So, I thought it was pretty. After two years, a sweet coworker asked me if I knew what that was.

They had probably made fun of me the entire time. They built their cubicles higher because I was too loud on the phone. Thinking back, they were complete jacka**es; I was just too busy to notice. I was there to support my three beautiful daughters and their increasingly expensive extra-curricular activities.

I was raised that no one ever does anything wrong. My father was an elder in a church. I grew up there with all my extended family. The church family. I was in the choir and went to church religiously for my entire childhood. I didn't have any idea that evil existed in the world.

Here I am perplexed, looking at these balled-up burnt pieces of foil in my schizophrenic daughter's dresser drawer. It had been a rough couple of years since she moved in. Medication, praying for answers, taking her to therapy, trying hot yoga, calling and calling and calling different programs where she may fit in.

Lonely, Marissa was so lonely. The cat helped, but she never took care of him. I resented having to do it. She had a friend, Cade, that came over sometimes to visit. He was sweet, and I knew him from my oldest daughter Naomi's high school class. He had been on one of her many cheerleading teams. I hoped Cade would help Marissa out of her loneliness. Looking back, I wish I had understood more about what was happening. Naiveness was a horrible thing in regards to drugs—a horrendous thing. When I questioned her, she got angry. Why was I going through her things? Hello? Voices tell you to hide food. I look around your room every time I get a chance. I glance at your journals for any "diagrams." I am your mother. I look because I love you. I look because I care.

She didn't like that I just gave her a look. She didn't want to answer. I wanted to know why I kept running out of spoons. I just kept having to buy more spoons. I was convinced the "voices" must have told her to bury them in a "special" spot in the yard. I even looked for the disturbed ground where she always smoked. Marissa started talking to several "voices" and not me and turned away. Even after years of medications, she never entirely stopped hearing the "voices." The "voices" changed. They shifted from one kind to the next, but she never stopped hearing them. Ever.

I went about looking things up online. The same week after Marissa's friend Cade had been there. She went out to smoke, and I ran to her room. I was more aggressive this time, and I really searched. Her mattress was an old wooden one with a fabric bottom. I noticed some of it was hanging down. That's when I found "the stash." It had a pipe and a lighter, a spoon, and a bunch of things I didn't recognize. It had an ominous, chemicals-and-body-odor smell. Because I had no idea what this was, I quickly took out my phone and took a picture. I put everything back and returned to my coffee. Despair crept in.

Later that day, I showed the picture to my husband. He had no idea either, but he had me send the picture to him. He knew someone at his work that had experience in that area. The next day my husband's buddy from work looked at the picture and said he thought this was burnt hash. I still had no clue. But after some research, I relaxed a little. At least it wasn't heroin.

Things with her had been complacent for about a year. She just complied with meds and remained sad. Very, very sad.

"Do you want to go to meetings? How about the gym?" I prompted.

Marissa would just blankly nod her unwillingness. In 2014, after two years of fighting this illness and a couple more trips to the mental hospital for stabilization, I had not discovered any recovery options. Nothing seemed to reach her. I had filled out all the highly complicated disability paperwork thinking there was no way she would get turned down with this much backup documentation.

Holding my breath, I read the paperwork from the yellowish envelope. If you've tried to receive benefits from the government in the United States, you know what I'm talking about. The vital mail comes in a yellowish envelope or has a prominent note on the outside. It depends on whether the notice comes from the state or federal government. Carefully, I opened the letter. The blah, blah, blah, determining blah, not to be eligible. My heart sank. I was praying she could get the help she needed through some government special disability magic. I prayed that it wasn't as much a fantasy as Marissa's Magicland.

My deadline was a couple of years away to make this happen. Once she turned twenty-six, I knew Marissa's medications would no longer be covered by her father's insurance. The insurance that paid for the three thousand dollars a month shot. After hiring an attorney to fill out the same exact disability paperwork, I waited another year and a half. With the deadline for the insurance coverage rapidly approaching, I desperately wrote to the manufacturer of the shot required to keep Marissa's mind from decompressing into psychosis. I begged and pleaded with my motherly transportation broker, negotiating, frantic, persistent.

I thought it would come to my retirement funds or the shot. I talked with my husband about the possibility that we may not have a choice. I was not going to let my precious Marissa's mind decompress over money. I would and could make more money. I couldn't make more of the good part of her brain. Understanding my urgency, the manufacturer sent me a letter three weeks later. It had a bunch of legal stuff, but at the end, it said: We will send one shot a month to the provider. Tears of relief streamed down my face. *Thank you, Lord. I know that was You guiding me.* I thought. She had to take that dose from the manufacturer twice.

Another six months later, two long years total. In October of 2015, I got the letter in a yellowish envelope. Not breathing, I read— Blah, blah, blah, blah, has been determined to be disabled. I read it again and again. You would have thought I would be happy to see this notice. It meant Marissa could continue to receive the shot. That disability would cover her other medications. That she would become eligible for a few hundred bucks a month to help with groceries and all the things she needed to survive life. It was a win, the prize.

I'd spent countless hours and stressful, sleepless nights trying to accomplish this goal. I just stared at the notice and couldn't blink or move. I put it back in its yellow envelope. I wrote in big letters with a blue sharpie on the outside: "Marissa's proof of disability." I was relieved the blue ink didn't bleed as my tears fell onto the letter— one after another. I didn't stop crying for several days. On and off, I sat at work and just saw those words of permanency echoing like a nightmare that was real. This was not going to get better. I was glad at that moment that I didn't know what was to come. I could not have gone on. Looking back, those were the good times. I wish I had known. I would have celebrated the good more often. I wish I had paid more attention to the little pieces of foil. Little things are sometimes big things. Good and evil.

Chapter Five

A FRIEND FOR MARISSA

O ne of the biggest struggles for schizophrenics is
socializing. Friends to hang with are a rare commodity.
So, in early 2016, when Marissa wanted to invite her friend
Rebecca over, I was thrilled. I had heard Marissa talk to her, and
she seemed really sweet and understanding of Marissa's
condition. Thankful to see a regular smile, I agreed to allow her
to come. I had restricted Cade after finding all the burnt pieces
of foil and stash.

I made a fruit and cheese tray, almost jubilant to have a
glimmer of hope. I allowed myself to dream. Maybe Marissa
could have a chance at normalcy if she made some friends.
Rebecca had beautiful blond hair and a sweet smile that seemed
to light up her entire face. She was innocent looking with shy
eyes and smelled as if she'd taken a shower in sweet pea spray.
She and Marissa laughed and went to her room. I heard them

listening to music and playing on the guitar. Normal stuff—my schizophrenic daughter had a friend over and was doing normal young adult stuff!

"Thanks for letting Rebecca come over," Marissa said giddily.

"I've never seen this version of Marissa. She's so bubbly." My husband said, amazed. "She comes off with some quirky lines, so funny." He added.

Rebecca fought with her mother, and Marissa asked if she could stay the night. Reluctantly, I agreed. Sometimes Marissa went down dark holes of the white witch, talking to dead people and controlling the line with her hand gestures when she was close to shot time. Marissa usually had episodes at night, and I was worried. She was due her once-a-month shot. It was scheduled for the next day.

I watched the clock and heard music and laughter. It reminded me of the many nights I listened to Marissa and her two sisters laughing and singing silly songs. They would make up elaborate plays for hours.

That night went well, and I dropped Rebecca off the following day at a different friend's house. She came over a couple of times a week for several months. Marissa had her regular episodes of "voices" and laughing and controlling the world with her hand gestures. Now they were milder and controlled. She loved having a friend to share in her life.

As the weeks of schizophrenic normal played out, it became like a tragic symphony. With its dramatic ups and downs, the feeling of the existence around her room became darker and darker. As if someone was dimming a light switch on Marissa's positive energy. I couldn't seem to understand my mother's instinct to protect. My mind was in full "protect my child" mode. I didn't really understand why. It was a heart-sinking, gut-wrenching feeling of evil manifesting, of a wickedness unraveling.

In April of 2016, Marissa hovered over me as I lay sleeping. "Mom, can I lay with you?"

What? That was my first thought as I opened up the covers to her. She had never done this before. Not since she was my innocent little girl. Certainly not since she had come to live with us. We had moved into a bigger house recently. I hoped that she would find peace in this new environment. She hadn't even been in our room before. Alerted by the sweat and her sense of terror, I smoothed her hair from her face and held her trembling hand.

Her voice quivered. "Mom, something just pulled me out of my bed. They were trying to take me! I felt them try to rape me."

What! I thought as I held her uncontrollably shaking shoulders. "Are you ok? Are they still here?"

My husband, overhearing our conversation, sprang out of bed and found his gun. He searched the house, every room, every corner. He even searched every corner of our vast basement. Nothing. She lay there next to me for the rest of the night, trembling.

"Don't you think you should tell someone about this at the hospital? Maybe your medicine is causing a weird side effect." I posed a possible scenario.

"No, no hospitals."

The next day I took off work and tried to help her make sense of the night before.

"I felt them grab my feet and pull me off the bed; they took me away to a damp kingdom, they tried to rape me. Mom, I'm so scared to go to sleep." Her eyes widen with terror.

I tried to console her as she lay next to me on the couch, curled up like a fawn in a mother's embrace. I felt like the Mother in Bambi protecting my child at all costs. The devil was not going to take my sweet little girl's dreams. I had to fix this, make a plan, go a different route. I prayed, *hedge Your protection over Marissa, Lord.*

Chapter Six

TACTILE DEPRESSION

Tactile, it's when schizophrenics start to feel hallucinations. Not only was she not getting better, but her illness was progressing. Despair mixed with anger crept in. Marissa was still hearing different "voices," seeing orbs of angels and demons. Now she felt hundreds of people raping her every night and screamed uncontrollably. All while being fully medicated. This was as good as she could be. At least she wasn't catatonic or psychotic.

I was amazed by my sweet Marissa's handling of her symptoms. Even though she knew she was sick, she tried so hard to go out in public. She would come with me to the grocery. She always had obvious symptoms. When she would do her involuntary schizophrenic laugh, she would apologize. I kept reassuring her, "I love your laugh." When people stared, I threw it in their faces. She skipped with me through the parking lot as we laughed like children. We're off to see the Wizard– We'd belt out while trying not to fall, attempting to cross our legs around each other. We would act out a scene from Good Burger.

I tried my best to add joy to her twenty-four-hour-a-day tortured life. I left positive notes on her plate. Got her inspirational journals to write in. Made special cupcakes with "I love you." I read about her illness and called one support group after another. But nothing joyful could be added to her tactile hallucinations. Nothing freed her– A wellspring of evil erupted from this torture chamber to form a very dark path.

Rebecca kept coming over even after the tactile events started. Little did I know she had her own darkness. There was a reason they were drawn together. Rebecca was the death of all things good in our home. Rebecca introduced my sweet little girl Marissa to the world of demons that some call drugs. The tactile hallucinations caused my precious daughter to reach out for any other form of escape. She couldn't sleep, rarely ate, the prescribed medications were no match to the villainous tactile addition to her symptoms.

I frantically searched for answers, continually calling and calling and calling different agencies and clinics and researching online resources. I wasn't able to find solutions or fix anything. Rebecca had just gotten out of jail and rehab. She had all the connections to the demons that appeared angel-like to Marissa. Darkness descended on my Marissa in the form of heroin.

Naiveness reared its ugly head again. At first, I just noticed my dresser drawers were shuffled around. I didn't really think anything of it. Maybe my stepdaughter was looking for something. Or my husband couldn't find his keys. Then I noticed an old sentimental bracelet lying on the closet floor from years gone by. *That's weird.* I thought. I hadn't touched that old jewelry box in years.

The next day was Sunday. I went to put on the unique necklace my grandmother had given me. I always wore it to church. Weird, I put it right back last week in the little box at the bottom of my dresser drawer. I searched all around and found the box in a different drawer. It looked as if to have been shoved under the socks in that drawer. For a brief moment, I was relieved. I must have been in a hurry. I thought. Slowly, I opened the ornate little box. Stunned at the reality that it was empty. I started looking around. My unique graduation cross from my great-grandmother was gone. My other great-grandmother's diamond earrings. The special aquamarine ring my mother gave me when I turned eighteen. All vanished.

Everything that was of value had been stolen. We did not make a police report because my daughter may have been involved. Betrayed and shocked by it all, I sat on the bed defeated, angry, confused. I let the tears come. Betrayal after spending countless hours and years was too much for me to bury. I wasn't making it to church. I walked into the kitchen, pulled out my IPA beer from the refrigerator, and stuck it in the freezer. This was not ok. Everyone else in the house just looked at me, and I could only wave them off.

J. *Mark Stacy*

"Go to church. I'll be ok." I said as they walked out the door.

The next day the security cameras were installed. I suspected Rebecca. She had just stayed three days straight as she had fought with her mother again. After that, my brain started working again. I remembered Marissa had taken sleep meds and was on one of her many two-day sleep cycles. I know these cycles well, and there's no way to wake her when she gets in these slumbers. Anyone with a mentally ill child will understand what I am talking about. Rebecca had acted alone.

Marissa had money of her own. Her disability account was empty. Since I was her payee administrator, I looked into the Uber account I had created with her debit card. It had been used over and over, and I knew Marissa hadn't gone to this many places. After canceling her card and updating everything one has to do when a debit card has been compromised, I attempted to talk to Marissa about what happened.

"Did you know Rebecca was using your Uber account?" I offhandedly asked.

"Yeah, uh, she got stuff for me, uh, I need stuff." She vaguely answered.

"I will cancel your Uber account if you let anyone else use it," I told her sternly.

"Uh, ok, well, it's my money; I need stuff." Marissa's hand dismissed me.

62

"We'll talk about it later," I added as I started to close her door. What is that smell? A different chemical scent mixed with year-old dirty socks. This was a new smell for her room. The typical old food and days-old unlaundered clothing were present. But this smell was unique in the disturbing triggers it brought back from my past with my daughter Elyse. It was the dark, ominous, lingering breath of addiction.

At this time, I didn't know my precious child was attempting self-medication. She found another friend who let her come to his house, and I was ok with it.

"Mom, uh, this is Sean."

He seemed kind and gentle, a little strange, but Marissa and strange always seemed to mix well. I was happy to keep her distracted. He wasn't Rebecca, and Marissa wasn't alone. He was a slight person with a crooked smile and had a look of blankness. Her beautiful fair skin and blue eyes made Sean fall hard for Marissa. Watching my Marissa holding hands with someone like a regular young adult brought me to tears.

At first, they seemed really happy. Maybe Sean can help her stop the tactile attacks. I allowed myself to be distracted from harsh reality for the moment. And try he did– in the form of a needle. My naiveness had failed Marissa again. Sean fixed Marissa by regulating her intake of heroin. Sean was an expert in the illegal drug world and had been in and out of jail. He was the one that would shoot up with her– over and over. He was death disguised as a pale, blue-eyed, blank-faced, red-headed boy.

Marissa was just happy to have "friends." She had become increasingly unstable with her evil episodes escalating. I had scheduled an extra trip to her nurse practitioner, and they prescribed Adderall to see if that would help stabilize her moods. When I went to get her dirty dishes the next day, I noticed the empty prescription bottle peeking out from under the bed.

When I questioned a half-conscious Marissa, she said, "yeah, someone took them."

She wasn't even supposed to have the bottle in her room. I usually kept all her meds together in my safe. I had younger stepkids and was very strict about where I kept medicine. I had just picked this prescription up and given it to her. I left it on the table since we didn't have the kids at the time. I started to piece things together.

Tragedy had struck my workplace. My boss of ten years was tragically killed. Stress and sadness at work had added to the impending doom that seemed to hover over our home. I was falling into a deep hole. A hole I'd spent years digging out of. A dark cloud followed me everywhere. Depression reared its head once again in my life. I had to fight. If I fell apart, I was no help to anyone. *Lord, please give me strength, help me know how You want me to handle this. Thank you for my many blessings, and you know the rest. Amen.* I searched for His light in this dark dungeon.

In my youth, I never felt good enough. My brother, on the other hand, was good at everything. My sister was the baby that could do no wrong. And me? I was the classic middle child. Google middle child syndrome, and that was me. My constant desire for things to go as planned. When I was going through my terrifying divorce, my counselor said I suffered from situational depression and PTSD. She said they were both understandable and that if I was feeling happy at that stage, she would have been troubled.

These diagnoses were not fun things to navigate when trying to walk through the depths of hell with a mentally ill child. Now, an addicted mentally ill child. Having watched my cherished youngest child Elyse struggle with addiction for the last ten years, I was devastated to face this in my precious Marissa, my middle child. Another trip winding down a harrowing, purely demonic path of destruction.

I wrestled with my own depression. My go-to was food. In high school, I had bulimia. I would get upset, take a box of Twinkies or whatever I could find, eat the entire package, bag, carton. Then go to the bathroom and heave it all up for an hour. It was self-punishment. I wasn't good enough to fix it, so I ate an entire bucket of chicken, a whole pizza. It was a horrible festival of self-loathing. I wasn't good enough to help her. Not when I couldn't even fix myself. The urge to get those dozen donuts was ever-present. Every day I wanted to do anything to punish myself for failing. I had failed yet another one of my sweet, innocent little girls.

What was I going to do now that she was addicted to heroin, happy with her friends, and asking me for money daily? I knew she was using the money to burrow down the hole to the demonic evil waiting eagerly to embrace her. Day after day, I tried to find a way for her to be rescued. I grounded her to her room only to watch helplessly as she allowed her "friends" into my house. I pulled them aside and told them if they weren't let in by me, they would have cops visiting them. I knew where all of them lived. I was no longer naive to what they were doing.

Marissa got angry.

She called the police on me. "My mom is holding me hostage." Again, I found officers in my home. I had the Power Of Attorney signed by Marissa and the hospital medical records.

I had to defend myself against her constant attacks. "I'm sorry, officer, I'm her payee, and she isn't doing good things with her money." What I wanted to say was: She spends all her money on her next fix, and I'm helpless against that evil fantasy release. She feels a thousand people rape her every night, and no one can seem to fix it.

Wearily, I went on day after day with no answers. "Please let me take you to the hospital." I pleaded with Marissa.

66

"No, uh, I'm better. Why would I need a hospital? You ok, mom? Yeah, you're scaring me. I need my money today, like all of it, ok, yeah."

She accused me of being crazy. She accused me of stealing her money. The last several years caught up to me in a moment. I broke.

Chapter Seven

BROKEN HOPE

I knocked on Marissa's door the next day as I held my breath. Secretly, I wanted her to be gone. Maybe she was just lost somewhere, and I don't have to do this.

She softly managed, "come in," with her "I'm wasted" voice.

I stood as tall as possible and tried not to tremble at the reality of the moment. "You have to leave." I stuttered, but I was stern.

She abruptly sat up. "What the hell are you talking about? You have my money. I'm not leaving; you have to take care of me. You ok, mom? I think you need the hospital."

I took a long draw-in. Breathe... "No, I don't." That's all I could say through my tears.

You might think these were tears of sadness. No, they were tears of anger! When anyone has turned to drugs, they are no longer a person. They are addicts controlled by their disease. Daughter or not, disabled schizophrenic or not, addicted was her new dominion. Addicts live in that deep chasm, and they strived on the evil that dwelled there.

"Get your things; I'm sure you have money in your account for Uber. I'll give you an hour, or I will call the police."

All my trigger alarms went off at once. Trigger from when I made her leave the first time. Trigger from her sister Elyse's hell on earth still playing its demonic symphony. I knew from experience that I was not able to fix an addict. Only the addicted can cure their addiction. No one could do it for them. Anyone else was the problem. The enabler. The end—period, exclamation mark.

It was silent for a few minutes. "Did you hear me?" I paused with my hand on the filthy door jam.

"Yeah, you will see the error of your ways. I am the master of all of Magicland and control the line. I will f*ck you from the land between, and you will know my wrath." Her voice was hush, monotone, deliberate, haunting. It ran through my bones, and coldness crept up my spine. Unable to breathe, I could feel the atmosphere shift. All the air collapsed, and it was chokingly still.

At that moment, my husband's rescuing voice echoed, "Babe, I'm home."

I turned from that wickedness and retreated to the kitchen, unable to grasp what I had just witnessed. It was worse than any nightmarish voice I had ever heard. And it echoed over and over in my subconscious. *Did I imagine that?* It was the devil's presence. This encounter with Marissa's demonic presence haunted my dreams. It wasn't just the voice this time. If only someone could save her from this evil. If only I would never again hear this voice. If only—

With an arrogant "goodbye, mom," she had one of her friends pick her up. She had taken all her meds with her as I was done helping her with anything. She had no way of making her doctor appointments, getting her shot. What will happen to her? Where will she live or get food? What if she decompresses without her shot? That wasn't my sweet daughter, I kept telling myself and repeating to myself. Nothing could have eased the agony of watching my drug-addicted daughter Marissa walk out the door. *When will I see her again?* The thought brought me to rivers of tears.

It was death, grieving, mourning, and the utter depths of despair. I would have given anything to go back to that little girl in her room with the laugh and the hand gestures. I wanted to fix this impossible scene playing out in my life. But I knew only Marissa could do that. The thought of an already unstable person trying to achieve such a task brought me to my knees. *Lord, please.* But I couldn't maintain the stamina to continue.

Darkness, death, dread was all-encompassing. It felt hopeless, a word that all mental health professionals are trained to ask. "Do you feel hopeless?" It has been well known as a suicide recognition word. I stopped caring or talking to anyone about anything. Hope was a stranger that betrayed me.

I would never harm myself, but that doesn't mean I didn't want to leave this earth. It hadn't been too kind to me. It took my baby five months into my third pregnancy, my innocence at the age of ten. It took my best friend, my life partner, when the world stole him and turned him into a monster that emerged when he drank. It took my youngest child at eleven to the world of addiction and my middle daughter at the age of twenty to schizophrenia. And now, this same child was addicted to the worst kind of evil.

It was such a long struggle to bring Marissa from the edge of darkness. It was hopeless to think she would escape the lure of fantasy's release. I wasn't angry anymore. I was numb— and the numbness terrified me. I continued with my meaningless job and tried to find happiness in my wonderful husband and terrific stepchildren. I helped my older daughter Naomi struggle with life decisions. *Lord, I need your strength.* I prayed as my numb mind searched for shelter.

I prayed frantically for my oldest daughter Naomi to stay on the positive side of our family's reality. It was so devastating. I had a big pity party for several months. I drank too much, ate

71

whatever I wanted, never slept, and worked all the time. I tried to distract myself in any way I could. I had to go on and manage my career, my life. There was no other choice. a cloud of despair hung there for those months like a robe of darkness. A heavy robe that is too hot after coffee, even on the coldest morning. A robe I was trying to shed. Desperately, I sought hope. *Lord, help me find the way.* I wrote these words on my desktop, refrigerator, and nightstand.

Chapter Eight

MIND FULL OF CHARACTERS

"**M**ommy, mommy, are you, my mommy? Can you come to get me?" At first, Marissa's voice was unrecognizable. "I think you need to take me to the hospital. Sean broke up with me, and I need you to take me to the hospital." Her childlike voice sounded angelic except for the words. "I want to die, mommy. Are you my mommy?" It was the voice of a child, a small child.

"Marissa?" I inhaled her name. I heard that she was living with Sean. For several weeks, there'd been only a few conversations between us that were all about money.

"No, who's Marissa? Is she pretty? Is she nice? Is she my mommy? Mommy, are you my mommy?" I could hear the phone tap on what I presumed was the counter and drop on the floor—shuffling of a conflict and a pause that seemed an eternity in my mother's instinct mind.

"Mom?" The familiar voice of my cherished youngest daughter Elyse brought me to tears. Marissa's friends were also Elyse's friends, and they had called her. "Mom, you need to come right now." I hadn't talked to my youngest for months, and for a moment, I let myself be glad to hear her voice. I secretly hoped for our relationship to mend somehow. But reality grabbed me quickly, and I had to decide— Do I go? Or do I stay in my numbness of despair?

As I arrived at the bowling alley's parking lot, I could smell the stale cigarettes through my cracked car windows. I wanted the fresh air, but this wasn't what I had in mind. As I went to roll them up, Elyse stepped into view. I leaped out of the car to greet her. No matter what, the love for your children never waivers. I hugged her like a mom hugs a soldier returning from war. A tear welled in her eye, and she was visibly relieved to see my reaction to her being there.

Marissa was sitting awkwardly on the curb outside the entrance to the bowling alley. Her head to one side, tinkering with a rock on the ground with her foot. Like a little child, she marveled in the world's wonder with innocence.

"I've been with her for two and a half hours, mom. She pissed me off at first, acting like a baby. But she's scaring me, mom." Elyse's eyes welled up with tears. "I don't think she knows me or who she is." Tears started running down her pale cheeks. "I asked if she wanted to call mom, and she said she got all excited and started mumbling. 'Mommy, you know my mommy?'." Elyse was visibly shaking now, "I told her you were my mommy too."

Marissa ran to me like a toddler who would go up to strangers to pick them up. She looked so innocent, and the bewilderment in her eyes was a twinkling I knew well. Marissa was so excited to meet me. She had no idea who I was. She kept up the "Are you my mommy?" dialog all the way to the hospital and the entire time we waited. Her friends really did care what happened, and I allowed my youngest and one friend to ride along with us. Secretly, I just didn't want to be alone in the car with Marissa. Someone needed to make sure Marissa didn't shift to the evil persona. When we got to the hospital, Elyse and the friend got a ride back to the bowling alley.

"Mom," but Elyse couldn't find words and collapsed into me.

"I'll take her in," I whispered as we shared the look of so many families of the mentally ill.

Going through the same process with the waiting and the blaring door. We finally got to the interior waiting area. It was just Marissa and me. She was still asking, "Are you my mommy?" when they called us to the intake evaluation room. A room we had been in at least twice a year for the last five years. It was ten by ten with all beige walls and one half glass-windowed door that automatically locked. Keys clanged in a constant crazed musical. All the doors were locked and clanged open and shut. It was a sad, lonely place where you felt the eeriness of mental evil all around. There was no hope in this intake evaluation room.

When they were finally done with the familiar paperwork, the friendly interviewer asked if we were comfortable and ready to begin. I almost laughed out loud. She started asking Marissa the usual questions. Blankly, Marissa stared into the beige wall of hopelessness.

"How old are you?" The interviewer asked.

Marissa paused with a look of a scared cub, then in her childlike voice, she stuttered. "I don't know...two?... uh... four?...is that right?"

Then the interviewer switched to me for answers, and I had them all. What's her drug of choice? What was her diagnosis? What was her living arrangement? When the questions were filled out, the door slammed shut. Jaded and exhausted, I glanced at my schizophrenic, helpless child.

Marissa was very quiet, very calm– too quiet– too calm. The reinforced locked door with half glass was across from her. She was staring at her reflection. For a few moments, she didn't move a single muscle. The familiar lack of air made me shift uneasily causing the chair to squeak and crackle. Noticing me for the first time, she sat up in a wild stance that startled me. A different voice emerged. Another person spoke.

Pointing at her reflection in the glass, the persona Marissa had shifted to said, "Who is that?" I don't think she was talking to me.

"That's your reflection, Marissa." As if I was in physics class answering world mysteries. I stammered at my nervous mistake. *Never let an unstable person see you be afraid.* I had read and discovered firsthand that it triggers some people with mental difficulty.

"I'm not Marissa! Marissa is dead! I hate Marissa!" Her shrill voice pierced the air. "I'm Christine; I'm not Marissa! Why would you say I'm Marissa? Marissa is dead! I killed her! I killed Marissa! I am not Marissa! I'm Christine!" Marissa shouted.

Terror grabbed me, and I felt myself hurtling toward the door. The interviewer, who had heard Marissa shouting, was already unlocking the door as I frantically rapped and cried out. "Let me out!"

I turned to my mumbling, twitching, schizophrenic daughter, who was now hysterically laughing as she dropped to the floor. She looked up at me with the eyes of a scared animal before being stuck. The fear in those eyes is the sadness that kept me from sleeping.

"I love you no matter what." Tears had to wait as I told my beautiful daughter, "it's going to be ok."

There, balled up crying then laughing on the dirty intake evaluation floor, I left my sweet Marissa.

A kind nurse asked me if I needed anything. Security had gone in the room with Marissa, and I didn't see what happened next.

"Help her." I pointed to the room and looked around at the other parents waiting. Their looks mirrored mine—despair wrapped in fear with sides of utter sadness and hopelessness.

It was then that the nurse said something that made me cry uncontrollably. "I'm sorry for your loss."

It was the first time that anyone acknowledged what I felt. Greif, loss, my child was gone. She wasn't coming back. There were many personas that Marissa took on over the years. She was a little child, a sixteen-year-old named Christine, a person named Jerrico There, and the evil. These are the ones that I know of. She would dress differently and talk differently whenever one of them would emerge. I didn't trust the evil, and I was praying for answers again. As much as I wanted to, I could not give up on my child. She was so sick.

For the next fifteen days, she was in the hospital and then tasked with thirty days of daily outpatient drug rehab. Ok, question. How is this person that voluntarily gave up driving because she sees things that aren't there going to get to an eleven am to two pm rehab every day? After years of watching this kind of thing unfold, the short answer was no one seemed to be able to do anything. Since their appearance and actions as a schizophrenic mimic a "tweaker," everyone judged them so harshly. Everyone except the few that understood they had no control over their illness or how it manifested. It's sadly jaded with no hope in the drug rehabilitation world for the mentally ill.

Marissa got back on the shot and promised to comply with treatment. I shuffled her during my lunch hour back and forth to rehab for thirty days. She was doing really well. She seemed to like rehab and started on her steps to recovery. She wrote in her journal every day and started the familiar laugh. We skipped through the grocery parking lot, and things went back to "normal." I still had the recurring sense of evil but, with time, that eased.

Another year went by. She was sent to a different hospital for another tactile episode in hopes they'd find some new treatment. Sadly, they didn't know how to manage the extreme hallucinations. But we had to try something different... something new, a different route.

She continued struggling with feeling the people raping her every night. She screamed and screamed and screamed. It was hard to maintain any peace. The police were frequent guests as she would get mad and call them. Tell them I was stealing money again. This time because I wouldn't get her the snacks that she wanted. She'd tell them I was locking her in her room when I wanted her to stay home when it was apparent she was having an episode.

Her Christine persona was a teenager and acted like it. Marissa's tactile hallucinations had her believing that people were coming into the house. She would barricade the door. We would have to go in through the window to get her out. This went on and on. But she didn't go back to heroin, not at first. We made sad trips to the mental hospital twice a year for stabilization and medication adjustments.

Loneliness set in. This was a war, and loneliness was the enemy. The emotion that's grasp was strong enough to cause a person to change course. It sucked the life of joyful people. There is no room for light to survive when they have no outlet. Darkness had a way in through loneliness. My sweet Marissa was a victim of this enemy.

I had not taken the cat to our new home, and she was without any friends once again. She continued to have episodes in public. I called and called and called one program after another. Again, I was told, "there's a gap when it comes to the mentally ill." Nothing stopped her tactile symptoms of "someone is pulling the skin over my eyes. I can't see." Or, "I can't hear anything, my ears are blocked." or the many, "It hurts, Mom, make them stop. Please, mom, make them stop."

I just wanted to drink my beer and go to bed. I just couldn't fix Marissa's illness. I called hospitals, clinics, and government agencies to see if she could get into a group home or go on some outings with other people. I tried to get her to go to NAMI meetings to meet other schizophrenics. Maybe if she sees that others with her same illness did the same things. Saw the same things. Felt the same things. Desperately, I wanted her to feel included, accepted. I wanted her to see most schizophrenics, in an attempt to appear "normal," learn to read lips. Most schizophrenics watched lips just like she did. Most of them hear multiple "voices" and constantly need to figure out where those "voices" originate.

They were so brave. I couldn't imagine what it was like living that way. Nothing saved Marissa from loneliness. The "voices" and people touching her weren't friends. They were her hell on earth. Nothing I found helped, no route, no way out of the dark cavern. No one could help find a way. Continually, I prayed for any solutions or rays of hope for the future of my middle daughter. Over and over, I was told, "there's a gap when it comes to the mentally ill."

Chapter Nine

LITTLE MIRACLE

"In July of 2016, Marissa had lived with us for almost four years. Her younger sister Elyse called with urgency in her voice. "Mom, I, I, really wanna, hm, well, need to talk to you about something." We had continued with our strained relationship with Elyse's addiction ever-present.

"Hi, of course," I answered, puzzled.

Not knowing if she'd be hungry, I made a fruit and cheese tray with her favorite butterfly crackers lining the edge. Like somehow, this food would have made this meeting seem normal.

"Do you want some root beer? I think I have your favorite kind." I implied that was unusual, but I always kept some hidden in the cabinet for her just in case she came over. My feet slightly wobbled as I hugged her frail body. Her face was drawn and pale. Her brownish green eyes reflected the same as when she was a little girl playing her first softball game. Her face lit up every time she would hurl the ball with her famous extra kick at the end. Such power built up behind her wall of a thin frame.

Like a stranger, she stiffly shuffled to my table. She sat down quietly and started to cry. Mumbling about the world of addiction and something about her boyfriend and a fight and something else, blah, blah. Elyse was drawn to drama. I listened, but I heard her ramble on about drama she mostly could have avoided for years. My sympathy for those situations had faded long ago.

She took a breath from her nervous introduction and finally got to the point. "Mom, I, I, I'm pregnant." She blew her words at me like they were on fire.

I just sat there stunned.

"It'll be ok." I lied as I hugged her tightly. Shocked, I was shocked. At that moment, my concern for her ever-present addiction took front and center. I knew she was still using drugs. Still living that demonic lifestyle. After a few minutes of listening to her sobs, I wrapped her in my robe, still warm from my stress-induced hot flash.

Draping it over her shoulders, I whispered. "It will be ok." How? My drug-addicted daughter is going to bring a child into the world. Panic! Inhale through the nose, exhale through the mouth. Leaning my head on her shoulder, "It's going to be ok." I repeated my earlier lie. I couldn't breathe out anything else. A plan, we needed a plan. My mind sprang to a thousand scenarios at once.

"Have you thought about what you want to do?" I held my breath. She was an adult, and for a moment, it terrified me that she was in charge of her own body. Sobbing uncontrollably, her little girl puppy dog eyes looked up at me.

"To live with you." Elyse fell into me as she said those words, not wanting to look me in the eyes.

All the air escaped my body. I'd spent years fighting with Elyse and dealing with her addiction. Every. Single. Day. When she left to live with her boyfriend, it was a relief. A relief I felt guilty about. Mother's guilt was like no other. How could I have given up? After years of doing the wrong things, I learned an addict has to want to get better. Only the addict could do that. This is how I learned anyone who tries is part of the problem. The enabler. Period. Exclamation mark.

I learned guilt was not a good reason to be part of the problem. I knew giving an addict money was like painting over a Rembrandt. Ruining their chances of ever getting back to God's perfect creation. Guilt was and is the enemy! It's all about you; your guilt couldn't help them. But it could hurt them more than anyone would ever know. I learned never to give an addicted person money, gift cards, presents. Nothing except food, perishable food you watch them eat. And water, only water.

So here I sat with my Elyse. Once shiny and brilliant, her brown hair was dull and smelled of old fast food grease. Anyone that has ever worked fast food knows that unmistakable smell. Rotten tomato mixed with old oil and sweat. Her drug of choice had escalated to heroin. Inhale through the nose, exhale slowly through the mouth. Breathe, just breathe. Plan...what is the plan?

I put my arms around her robe-covered shoulders, and we both sat there in silence. My dogs jumped up in our laps, and we stroked their necks, trying to ease the discomfort of this awkward conversation.

"Ok, we need a plan." I finally said. "There will have to be strict rules," is all I could come up with. I had to really consider all the factors. I couldn't do that and be objective and unbiased with my grandchild in her frail body. I needed to pull my husband into this conversation. Our marriage was a partnership. We were going to have to figure this out together.

"I want to do right by the baby, Mom." Elyse's eyes had a genuineness that I had never witnessed.

"Are you hungry?" I just didn't know how to respond.

"No, my ride's here to pick me up," she said while she glanced at her phone.

"Ok, I'll call you tomorrow." I hugged her and watched her walk out the door.

Hot, it was so hot! I pulled my bathing suit over my now bulging body. A body I didn't recognize from the fit person I had once been. Menopause and stress and allowing myself to eat whatever had taken its toll. My self-worth was gone. I struggled every day to just get out of bed. That ominous dark cloud followed me everywhere. My self-loathing festival of binging was ever-present. Not giving in to these urges must be what addicts go through, only on a much larger scale.

I admired recovered addicts more than anyone could know. Their journeys were so harrowing. Addiction could happen to anyone. Recovery must be like coming back from demon pools of hell with its constant lure of fantasy release. I've seen this first hand, but I still can't imagine having the strength to keep pushing through such a strong pull. The devil liked to win. In my confused state, I decided a swim might do me good.

We had this fabulous inground pool, an oasis. Our backyard was a beautiful, spa-like paradise. I'd worked my entire life to achieve this place. My crowning glory for the years tolerating rude customers and upset drivers. Years of that meaningless job had turned into this oasis of a yard. The hot tub had lights and the gazebo with its elaborate stone fireplace. Comfort. I had strived to feel comfortable my entire life.

I plunged headfirst into the depths of this crowning masterpiece. The water was warm, and I had spent several hours making sure it was clean before putting my suit on. I had my cold IPA beer close at hand, and I fluttered back and forth like a child. My husband had come home and saw me. He threw on his trunks, came out, and jumped in with the same jubilance. For a brief moment, I let myself be happy, and I smiled, watching my husband flutter around. Life was good.

Deciding to wait until later to talk about how to handle Elyse's news, I just splashed around. My oldest daughter Naomi and her boyfriend, my sister and niece all joined us, and we had the most beautiful night. We laughed and played Apples to Apples. I took the time to celebrate the good. I looked around at the smiles and listened to the laughter created by this beautiful oasis. It's going to be ok. Keep celebrating the good.

A child is a miracle of nature. I studied to be a nurse in college. All those millions of reactions to just stand. The coordinating muscles, tendons, and organs all worked together to balance. It was extraordinary! A magnificent ballet of universal elements all worked together. I thought how wonderful it would be if society was like that. All these coordinated efforts to achieve the incredible goal of balance. The body's enormous ability to grow a human in their body until they could sustain air independently. It was miraculous.

The next day was Saturday. With all those thoughts of the little miracle on my mind, I caught myself dusting the shelves of the extensive built-in entertainment center. Anyone that knew me would understand that wasn't something I did unless I was really nervous and wanted to keep occupied. I tried to approach my husband with this news. *What was I going to say?* My thoughts rambled to different scenarios. I couldn't choose the best way to handle this delivery of news.

I want to let Elyse live here. She's pregnant? I thought as I decided to stay with my usual direct approach. Straight to the point and direct. Questioning if that was a good way to introduce this hurtle had kept me up even after a few beers. With all the chaos of our household already bustling, I didn't know how this news would come across. I knew my husband very well, but this pushed boundaries I knew he wouldn't like.

Plan in hand, we sat at the table. I inhaled and paused to look at my husband. "Elyse is pregnant." I exhaled the words. He seemed shocked by the news and even more shocked that she had wanted to stay with us. "She's pregnant and wants to do right by the baby," I repeated myself. His eyes looked deep into my soul. He had a way of understanding my thoughts and not just my words. He saw the longing in my eyes—the ever-present need to be there for my children.

He took a long, deep draw of air. "Ok, I'm ok with what you're ok with." Simple as that.

"I love you, my husband." I kissed him, and I gazed into his brown eyes that wanted nothing more than my happiness. (And to go fishing)

It was agreed. She would live with us with strict rules. The plan and the regulations were laid out for Elyse to understand:

-Mom will go with me to all my appointments.

-Mom will hold and administer all my medications.

-Absolutely no visitors allowed.

-No other medications that aren't prescribed.

"Elyse, we talked and agreed you can live here, but you'll have to agree to the rules." I rattled off when I phoned her.

"I promise, I want to do right by my baby." She whimpered in relief.

Elyse Mark. She signed as I wanted it in writing to put on the wall for her to see. I drove her through town as she gathered what little garbage bags of stuff she had scattered around the couch hopping circle where she'd lived. Once again, I had readied a room. I led my cherished youngest Elyse to the front bedroom on the opposite side of the hall from her sister Marissa's.

"Mom, thanks for letting me stay here." Elyse's tears dripped on the hope chest made for her by her grandfather. A TV was set up with Netflix already logged in. This was a new start. A child is a blessing, no matter what. "This is amazing." She hopped on the bed, burying herself in the clean, soft covers.

"I want this to work. I love you no matter what." I reassured her as I kissed her forehead. "Get some rest. You and the baby need it." I encouraged her. I sat on the edge of the bed while my little girl fell fast asleep. Dripping tears and trying not to sniffle, the harsh reality grabbed me that Elyse hadn't had a bed of her own for years.

My thoughts drifted to Marissa. She seemed unaffected by the recent household changes. All she wanted to do was be with her new friends.

"Elyse is going to have a baby," I told her.

"Oh, cool." Marissa dully dismissed my words, and I wondered if she really understood. The household was bustling, and our lives started a new chapter—one day at a time.

Chapter Ten

HATE

My beloved oldest, Naomi, blessed me with a granddaughter. She was pure joy. They had just decided to move to California from Kentucky, and my heart was broken. Even though I genuinely wanted what was best for them, I was devastated. My granddaughter was pure joy. We had spent many hours nearly every day snuggling. She was about to turn one. I couldn't help but be excited at the thought of another joyful baby. No matter the circumstances.

The first doctor's appointment was the same week Elyse moved in. The nurse was really sensitive to our situation. I was so proud of Elyse for looking them straight in the eyes and admitting she was an addict. Neither of us realized what was to come. Did you know that if you were already addicted to heroin, you have to stay on it if you get pregnant? Did you know that withdrawal would kill the baby? It would kill the baby—It echoed through me like a knife. What? I had no idea. In my naive state, I didn't even think to ask if they would prescribe the substitute version of heroin that she would have to take.

The next day, at lunch, sitting at my desk with my heated up bowl of soup, I called the doctor's office to inquire about prescriptions. The substitute they had stressed she must stay on.

With a monotone voice, this person at the desk said. "Oh, we don't prescribe that kind of thing." *Wait, they don't prescribe the medicine my daughter needs to keep her baby alive?* I thought.

"Doesn't she have to take that, or the baby will die?" I strained to hide my panic.

"All I know is we don't prescribe that kind of thing." She blandly answered.

I thought she must be mistaken, so I asked to talk to the understanding nurse that had taken our information. After a long wait, the nurse came on the line.

She said, "I'm so sorry, we can't prescribe that type of medication. You'll have to get an appointment with a clinic, and I know sometimes they don't have appointments for several weeks."

What? What are you saying? I just couldn't comprehend this. In the calmest voice I could, I laid out my position to them. "Let me get this straight. You told us the baby would die without the heroin or substitute. But you don't prescribe that type of medication, and you didn't tell us? What you are saying is I have to **choose** to give my daughter money to get this medication illegally or let my grandchild **die**?"

After a very long pause, the monotone voice trembled, "I'm so sorry." With a sniffle, she gave me some numbers to call.

My coworker, who couldn't help but hear, burst into tears. I dropped the phone to the ground— I looked at her as I walked out the door gasping for air, muttering, "I'm going to need a minute." After three times around the large strip mall parking lot. The same lot where my schizophrenic daughter Marissa's tap dance episode happened, I stopped crying. No one should ever be in this position; I was very much against drugs of any kind! I hated them—a word I don't use lightly.

Never say never. I knew that I would be on my innocent grandchild's side. The child was the victim.

"Do you know where you can get Subutex?" Again, a direct approach was used as I glared at my daughter, filled with resentment toward her addiction.

Wide-eyed, Elyse's jaw dropped. More tears dripped onto the comforter as she couldn't be consoled for several minutes. "No, mom, I can't go back there, no." she sobbed.

"It's the only way. I'm sorry. I couldn't get an appointment for a month. It would have been two, but I paid the fifty buck deposit to hold the date and time." I explained, trying not to add my anger to her emotions.

She gathered the intel on where to find the substitute. I told her she wasn't leaving my sight with money, so she arranged the exchange for a public place where I could see. Reluctant wasn't a strong enough word for the discomfort of sitting in that place.

To go to these lengths as necessary? That was crazy. What the hell was I doing? I thought. The baby, I had to think of the innocent child that had no one else but us. I couldn't let my grandchild die. Overwhelmingly, I was already protective of this child. It was a feeling that emanated from a celestial place. A sense that remained ever-present. It was my job to protect my grandchild no matter what—a sacred duty.

Somberly, she moved slowly back to the car. I could tell she was humiliated by having her own mother watch her buy drugs. Good! I prayed that she would never want to do drugs again.

As she got back in the car, my eyes darted all around, and it reminded me of the time I picked my sweet Marissa up from her dad's ratty apartment complex. I drove away as she took the Suboxone out of her pocket and handed it to me. It was little foil sleeves that looked like something you have teeth whitening strips in. I pulled out the baggie as if it was purgatory and tried to decide the safest way to hold on to these highly dangerous illegal foil sleeves of hell.

The appointments with the pain management doctors were Walmart-at-midnight, meets Wall-Street-jungle, meets nursing home. Recovering addicts have to get their prescriptions from these doctors. So do patients with painful long-term conditions. It was a circus of withdrawing toxic actors. The smell of chemicals meets those year-old socks from my schizophrenic daughter's closet.

"Did you have to pay fifty bucks to get an appointment?" I asked an elderly man next to me. He just nodded, not wanting to talk to anyone in the lobby.

The staff at these offices didn't care or were just really jaded. If you missed your appointment, too bad. You had to show up ten minutes early, have all the paperwork filled out correctly, or too bad. No one seemed to care. The doctor wouldn't let me be in the room, but Elyse said she told him the truth, and he wrote the prescription.

The plan began. I would pick up the prescriptions for both Marissa and Elyse, spend my lunch hour every single day checking on them, and give them whatever doses. Day after day, it became routine. I started packing my gun again. Carrying around a highly sought-after substance in the illegal drug world is dangerous. I felt it my duty to discreetly and safely protect myself and my family. I was trained on my weapon and an expert shot. I took self-defense and made sure I was aware of my surroundings at all times. This was war. Evil existed, and it was everywhere.

Elyse was still drawn to the darkness. She would disappear for a couple of days at a time. Since I gave her Subutex every day, I didn't know where she could be going and why she would risk her child's health. Ever-present tension was in the air. Imminent danger lingered. I felt it all around me, but I dismissed it as paranoia. After all, this was a messed-up position to be in.

Elyse burst through the door screaming after being gone for three days. "Mom, I need you," she cried out. *What the hell?* My mind raced to a thousand scenarios. She went into this long ramble about "a guy" and blah, blah, "she owed," and blah, blah… and then she said, "he knows where we live, mom."

I didn't tell anyone about what unfolded next. I wish I could erase the next several hours of our lives. I was not allowing any drug dealing maniac to come to my house. "Arrange a meeting," I told her.

My daughter's shocked eyes met mine. "What? Mom, these are not nice people to deal with."

"They haven't met me. No one threatens my family." I stared her down. In my lifetime, I've been angry a lot. But the anger I felt this night was quiet— too quiet. It was deliberate, shameful. I walked to the car with Elyse in tow. Tucking my thirty-eight revolver into the holster, I laid it in plain sight next to the cup of day-old coffee.

"Mom, we can't just go there." She pleaded.

"Why not? The guy wants the money you owe him, right?" I pulled out my wallet and threw a hundred on her lap.

It felt like we were some gang members about to go on a shoot-out. I remember thinking. *Well, I have already seen Elyse in an orange jumpsuit in juvie. The worst that could happen is they kill us; oh well,* was my frame of mind in the car driving to meet "the guy." I looked at my four-month pregnant daughter sitting in the passenger seat. My body was tense from adrenaline and poised for war. Rage was in charge.

Abruptly, I started shouting at her. "I hate you for this! I hate you! I hope they blow my head off while you watch. I want them to just kill me!"

I meant it. In my brand new black Subaru, I pulled up to the gas station in the worst part of town. I had just picked this new car up from the dealer. This was the first time Elyse had even ridden in it. New car smell was quickly replaced as I rolled down the window to the odor of gas and tar and residue of broken lives.

Blankly, she stared at me. "Go on." I waved her out the door. Her tight tank top was now too short for her bully bump that shone in the sun as she walked away.

This is my life. Disbelief and rage hit me at once. Several groups of broken children walked by. I hung my hand out the window while holding my loaded thirty-eight revolver in my lap.

Not my daughter, not my house, not my family. I was not playing around. I had grown weary of being afraid. Elyse bolted out of the gas station door, eager to get out of there.

"Well? Are we good? You want me to talk to him?" I mocked, glancing at the still visible weapon.

Wide-eyed, she quickly assured. "We're square, mom. Let's go." Gesturing me with her hands. "He's not a bad guy; he had his kid with him. He was just protecting his interest."

It took all my restraint not to punch her in the face. I hated her again. Pulling onto the street, an officer watched us drive away. I nearly waved at him with my revolver in hand, a reflex from my suburban life where we always waved at neighborhood patrols.

We were both silent for the half-hour drive back home. I wanted to kick Elyse out and never talk to her again. I hated myself for screaming the truth of the moment at her. I was ashamed of her, of myself. Exhaustion took over the adrenaline rant as I pulled into the drive of my beautiful home. The neighbor waved hello like the world was his oyster, and the roughest part of his day was enduring the heat while he watered their perfect front yard.

While my beer was tucked in the freezer, I returned my revolver to its hiding spot. "Anyone home?" My voice echoed in the tall ceiling of the dining area. A friend had picked up Elyse, and I found myself alone. Pulling open the door, I retreated into my oasis backyard. In one long gulp, I emptied my cold IPA. With my jeans and tee-shirt heavy with angry rage, I plunged into the deep end of the pool. Slowly, I sank to the bottom. Pausing at the stillness. I opened my eyes to the light above. Calm, weightless, peace surrounded me. *Lord, please forgive me. I am so thankful for my blessings. Please, Lord, protect us.* I prayed.

Bubbles escaped as I forced myself to linger longer than my breath allowed. Closing my eyes, a vision shocked my existence. A poster I'd once seen of Jesus dipping His hand in a pool. In that instant, I heard His merciful voice. "I got you." I heard it as clear as a mountain stream. Trembling out of sheer shock, I felt a warmth in my bones. Bubbles were all around. The water was airy, and His light shone all around me. Clenching my fists, I planted my bare feet and pushed from the bottom. I surfaced with a newfound rebirth.

Hope, it's so hard to find in these moments of such despair. His present launched me to the top. Dripping with renewal, I bowed my head. *Thank you, Lord. Thank you for sharing your strength. I am not worthy, Lord.* It was the end of a very long day.

Still soaking from my plunge, I ordered a pizza. Everyone would be home soon, and I had nothing to eat for dinner. I went on with the business of life. The hatred I felt on that road trip to the drug dealer's world remained ingrained in my mind like a minus thirty-degree tire. Made for a bumpy ride. In Alaska, if the temperature dipped below negative thirty, the air in your tires would lose pressure and become flat on the bottom. They knew they were in for a bumpy ride while their tires warmed as they went. Would I warm up? What was I capable of? I worried this feeling would never leave. Little by little, the hand from the pool faded the hate in my heart. It became less of me and more of a feeling. Time heals all wounds. At least that is what I've heard.

Chapter Eleven

PRAYING FOR DAYS

O n January 4th, 2017, I was sleeping beside my husband in our king-size bed at eleven pm. It had been another horrible day in the transportation world. Startled, I opened my eyes to my thirty-six-week pregnant Elyse hovering over me.

"What's wrong?" I asked. *Remain calm*, I told myself as I tried not to panic.

"Mom, my back and head are killing me. I took Tylenol like you said I could about half an hour ago, but something is wrong– I can feel it."

Blurry turned to concern, and I burst out of bed. Mom mode kicked in, and it was go-time. The doctor had been concerned about Elyse's deteriorating health at the previous visit. The nurse warned her blood pressure was elevated and said to watch out for headaches. Elyse and I made the decision together to go to the hospital.

Elyse had struggled with the Subutex and succumbed to her addiction throughout her pregnancy. Even though she knew heroin was coursing through her veins, she never missed a single obstetrician appointment. Since Elyse tested positive from her first visit, Child Protective Services were ever-present in those months. Elyse loved her baby, and she tried to do what was right. I prayed for her and the baby every single day. I never stopped encouraging her to choose the right path.

Once checked into the hospital, alarms blared loudly as they attempted to take her blood pressure. More alarms blared.

Nurses ran into her room. "We need to prep her now-" I overheard.

"What's going on?" Elyse's pale face was swollen, her hands trembling. "Mom, what's going on?" She repeated.

"I'm trying to find out. It's going to be ok; hang in there." I stroked her hair and smoothed the side of her face. The nurses couldn't keep the constant blaring to stop and finally silenced the machine completely.

"Her blood pressure is dangerously high, and we're trying to stabilize her." My brow contorted at what the nurse said as I watched them quickly insert an IV. "We're prepping her for surgery, her placenta is breaking down, and we need to get the baby out now." The look of panic on the nurse's face was my first indication that something was terribly wrong.

From the time we walked in the door to the time they had her in the operating room was less than half an hour. She was dying. The baby would follow if they didn't do something quickly. Her organs were shutting down, and her placenta was failing. My mind couldn't hear any more of this language, and I went numb for a moment.

As they rolled her out the door, I barely got a brief hug and whispered, "it will be ok." as I kissed her forehead.

They hurriedly gave me a gown. "Quick as you can, put this on, and these gloves and mask." The gentle nurse's assistant aided me. "I don't know if you'll be able to go in the room, but just in case."

Peering in the slit in the glass door, I saw them fly sheets over Elyse like sails in the wind. I helplessly watched the surgical team hovering over my sweet little girl and grandchild. I couldn't breathe. I couldn't move. I just prayed. *Please let them be ok. Lord, please.* No time for tears as I peered and gasped for air at the sheer terror in my mind playing demonic messages I was blocking with prayer.

The nurse looked at the door and nobbed side to side, indicating that I couldn't enter. Breathless, I saw them cover Elyse's face with the oxygen mask to put her to sleep. I felt the presence of God. I felt His grace and mercy upon me. I closed my eyes and lifted them to Him.

Thirty seconds, it was only thirty seconds later– I heard the most miraculous, melodious sound on the planet. "Waah, waah, waah." I recognized it instantly. It was the sweetest sound I'd ever heard. There he was! Through the slit, I saw them hold him up. He was bigger than I had envisioned for being premature and the lifestyle he had been subjected to. He was a brave soldier from the start. The nurse saw me through the slit and held him up to allow me to snap a picture. A treasure that captured this miracle.

My thoughts turned to my seemingly lifeless daughter. I couldn't tell if she was breathing under the sails. The lack of panic of the staff around her was my only indication that she was just sleeping. The nurse came out and said they had to put Elyse to sleep for her safety.

They whisked Adam away quickly as his oxygen numbers were low. Panic set in. I just wanted to hold him. They kept him in the incubator for warmth. He had tubes up his little nose for oxygen.

The staff noticed my furrowed brow and motioned to me. "You can reach in and hold his hand."

Slowly and gently, I reached out to my grandchild for the first time. His little body was not as pink as most babies I'd seen before. I was amazed at how well he looked, all things considered. When my hand reached his palm, I stroked it gently. His hand is open. I remember thinking how strange that seemed as most infants have tightly closed fists. I relished in his tenderness. The smell of disinfectant couldn't conceal the sweetness of my brave little grandson. Instinctively, he grabbed hold of my pinkie. Tears of joy drip one after another after another. It was an instant connection.

"I got you, little man, I got you," I whispered. Pausing, I closed my eyes and prayed for him to gain the strength God had given me. As I stood there, he opened up his tender eyes and looked my way. They say infants can't see very far, but I knew Adam was searching for me. In his eyes, I could see he recognized my voice. Simply mesmerized, I stood and marveled at this tiny miracle. I stayed by his side, holding his hand as long as the staff would allow.

My concern returned to my daughter. They had told me while I was with Adam that Elyse was being moved to a labor/delivery room. They couldn't get her blood pressure to stabilize, and they wanted her hooked to the monitors. I shuffled back and forth between my daughter and Adam for eight long hours. She hadn't woken up. Her blood pressure still wasn't stable. Adam was still on oxygen and under the lights. I was torn on where to spend my time. My husband's concern turned to me, and he tried to get me to take a break. Coffee was my friend.

Other family members shuffled in and out. No one else was allowed to go in with Adam. But they could see him, and they all marveled at him. He was large for a four-week premature infant at five pounds and one ounce and seventeen inches long. He was a born fighter.

After almost nine hours, Elyse opened her eyes, which immediately filled with panic. I couldn't imagine what it would have been like to be put to sleep, not knowing if my newborn infant would make it. Immediately, I pulled out my phone with the video of him holding my finger.

Joyful tears welled up in her bloodshot eyes. "My boy, oh my God, he is beautiful!

Tears flowed down and covered her gown, moistening the tape attaching the monitor to her chest. Alarms blared once again, and a nurse came in. Elyse's blood pressure was still out of control.

"Oh, my baby boy." She watched the video over and over.

Adam's oxygen level had stabilized, so when the nurse heard Elyse was awake, she rushed down to wheel him to her room. Holding him was a precious honor, and I made sure no one else other than me held him before his mommy had the chance.

"Someone wants to meet you." I leaned over to sit the tiny infant into her frail arms.

"Hello, little man. I'm your mommy. I love you so much… sooo, soooo much." She sat with her baby boy in her arms a couple of inches from her face and just stared at him. A calm I had never experienced regarding Elyse came over the room. It was a beautiful snapshot in time I will never forget. A precious, still moment. A rare, happy moment. Joy was all around, and all was right in the world, for that brief pause. There had never been a question that Elyse loved her baby with all her heart.

On the third day, Elyse was still in labor and delivery. They could not get her blood pressure stabilized. They brought Adam in, and we took turns holding him. I walked along the way as they led him back to the nursery for testing. I watched them give him the NAS test, Neonatal Abstinence Syndrome. He had started having a strange twitching. I'd never forget this day.

Marg marched into my daughter's room, the director of Child Protective Services for our area. She said blah, blah, blah, "we're taking custody of him. He needs special care for his condition, so we are transporting him to the NICU at the hospital in Louisville."

Louisville? I thought. *They're taking him away?*

"We'll bring him in so you can say your goodbyes."

What? We were both stunned.

"You will be able to visit him there." She handed us a plain white card with a handwritten number. "I will call you when he is settled."

The box they had him in for transport looked like a case you put explosives in. I couldn't believe this was happening. My daughter's face was tormented and twisted, and she couldn't breathe.

Struggling not to pass out, she held him tightly, "I'm so sorry I failed you, my sweet little man. I'm so sorry." The weight of the situation caused her to feel faint, and she motioned to me.

Holding him against my heart, I whispered in his little ear, 'I love you no matter what. I will be here for you no matter what. I got you, be a brave little man." I watched as they placed him in the tomb-like chamber for transport.

Inconsolable, we both sobbed. We were both shocked at the reality of the situation. Different darkness could be felt in the air. A fearful sadness I had never experienced. Time on the clock ticked, and the tv was no distraction.

When Elyse's phone registered "CPS," I answered as she was asleep. "He's in Section H. It's on the opposite side of the hospital." The director gave me instructions on how we could visit. It was two more long days before Elyse's blood pressure stabilized enough for her to be released.

The chair. I remember the chair in the NAS area of the Neonatal Intensive Care Unit was so cold and hard. I sat, struggling to see. Neonatal Abstinence Syndrome babies were cared for in dark dungeon-like rooms of despair because they are sensitive to light. The babies had a distinct weary cry. Mostly, I saw foster parents trying to comfort these babies, or volunteers, or grandparents—all with the same fearful sadness in their eyes.

Every grandparent, like me, had their child hanging in the balance, teetering on the edge of the dark drug world. My daughter and Adam were both hanging on to the ledge. Adam clung to me while I held him as long and as often as I could. His frail little body had wires hanging from his chest, hands, and feet. He melted into me for comfort, and I fed him his bottle. Innocent and sweet, he held my pinkie while I noticed his furrowed brow. His tremors were fierce, but so was his resolve. He was such a brave little warrior.

Almost three weeks into his treatment, the discharge plans were made. He was going to live with us, and Elyse was going to be monitored by CPS on a "reunification plan." It was all set. The nurse that morning thought it was strange that he had started running a temperature. He should not have a temperature. They ordered some tests.

I had never been so grateful. When the nurse pulled his spinal fluid, it was cloudy– Spinal fluid is supposed to be clear. With further testing, it was determined he contracted **bacterial** spinal meningitis. If we had taken him home... I shuttered. They immediately moved him to the NICU isolation unit. A vast room compared to the tiny NAS baby area. A team from the CDC had been alerted, and hell broke out.

The next few hours were a blur. Nine members of the CDC stood before me as I held Adam's frail body. They explained that they had to isolate what bacteria was causing this.

They talked about broad-spectrum antibiotics and blah, blah. When they said septic, my heart sank. I went to school to be a nurse and knew sepsis leads to the unthinkable. Organs shut down. His chances for survival showed on their faces. The doctor tried his best to keep the concern from his voice as he tried to explain in "doctor" talk.

The following day, I went through entering the isolation area. Gown, mask, gloves, check. The chill from the room made me rub my hands together to try to make them warmer. Slowly, I navigated through the wires that encircled Adam. As if he would break at the slightest jerk, I gently picked him up. Such a brave little man, so pale, so lifeless. His brow was deeply furrowed.

Like a treasured artifact, I held him in my arms and whispered, "I love you so much. God's got this. Be strong."

My daughter was supposed to be there any minute, and I stared at the door. Elyse hadn't spoken since they said his chances were slim. For the next nine straight hours, I shifted my gaze between this tiny, frail infant and the empty hallway. It was the longest day of my life.

When my husband came in, I asked if he had heard from her. "Not a word," was all that he said.

The doctors isolated the bacteria, E.coli, and they started aggressive treatment. The staff was so impressed with Adam's stamina and will. Mandatory three weeks of intravenous

110

antibiotics. Since he was so small, the IV had to be put in a vein on his head. It was a horrifying sight. I hated to see him go through so much. Daily he improved, but they warned of complications. He may not walk. He may not hear, have behavioral problems, and develop spina bifida. He has a large hole in his heart. He has a tethered spine.

Adam was improving daily, and that is what mattered. My daughter had shown up at the hospital the next day after his prognosis. I wanted to hug her and punch her at the same time. She didn't stay more than a couple of minutes. My heart sank as I knew the "hey, have any money I could borrow? I just wanna get something to eat" speech. I tried my best for this innocent baby's sake to think positive.

Two days: It was amazing how two days affected the rest of your life. Two days before Adam was cleared to be discharged from the hospital, I got the call.

"This is Child Protective Services. We need a meeting to discuss Adam."

"Babe, CPS says they need us to come at three o'clock to their office over by the grocery store," I called my husband concerned.

"What's going on? Is Adam ok?" My husband asked. Our immediate concerns were for Adam's health. We had just fed him and went over the discharge plan.

"I have no idea. CPS required Elyse to be there." I breathed heavily into the phone.

The receptionist at the CPS office looked at us sideways. My husband and I signed in on the tiny clipboard that the attendant quickly grabbed. "I'll let them know you are here. Anyone else showing?"

"My daughter is supposed to be here. I'll call her." I picked up my phone and dialed.

"Mom, I, I, I'm on my way. Sorry, sorry, I just got stuck in traffic. I had to drop my friend off first." Elyse stammered.

The director ushered us into her tiny office. "Is Elyse here?" She inquired.

"She's on the way, said she was in traffic," I said like a schoolgirl who had been accused of breaking the rules. I gazed at the scuff marks of despair on the walls and the obvious indentation of a doorknob.

"Is Adam ok?" I blurted.

"Oh, yes, I saw his report, and he seems to be thriving." My husband and I both sighed in relief.

"What's going on? Why are we here?" My husband asked calmly.

"I was hoping to have Elyse here, but I'll start the process with just the two of you. I have to do that anyway. Speak to you separately that is." She flipped through a million papers piled neatly on her desk. One by one, she sifted through them until she came to the one she wanted to show us. Inhaling with disgust and concern, she exhaled. "She tested positive for heroin. Adam can't go home with her." The words echoed, and for a moment, I didn't know what she meant.

Looking up at us over her reading glasses, she breathed, "There are two options here. We assign him a foster parent, or a relative foster could take custody." She paused and interlocked her fingers as if praying, or maybe it was a nervous gesture. "Are you willing to take custody of him?"

My husband and I startled each other, nearly yelling without any hesitation. "Of course!"

She smiled awkwardly. "I was hoping you'd say that," she added. "The biological mother will be allowed to stay in the home, but the baby must only be in your care. The biological mother will have to submit to regular testing. If she fails even one of those, are you prepared to make her leave? Let me stress that you will be required by the court, under oath, to abide by that ruling."

Without hesitation, we both answered. "We understand."

Frantically, we filled out the foster parent paperwork. Two days until Adam was set to be discharged. Two days to get full background checked.

Sign here and here, "I made you an appointment for the fingerprinting since it has to be done today." The CPS director stressed. And she gave us the address to go on our way home.

You have to be here (giving us another address) to sign more paperwork at ten am tomorrow, or they will not be able to get the background check done in time. You must attend this class at four pm. At seven pm you have to participate in this class. You must have certificates from both.

"Do you understand?" The director saw the overwhelmed look on our faces. "I will explain this to Elyse when she arrives. Thank you for stepping in." She added, leading us out of the room.

As we pulled out of the parking lot, we passed Elyse frantically parking. I was so relieved she hadn't noticed our car. Saving Adam from going into the foster system was going to be my only focus. My husband and I had a mission to pass the foster parent program in two days.

Sitting on our leather couch, you could hear every rustling. Ding dong and the pizza arrived. We both picked at the pieces on our plate. I watched my husband pacing and looking at the clock every two minutes. Both of us were waiting for the phone call to let us know if we'd been cleared. I was horrified at the thought that I wouldn't know where my brave little soldier was living.

When my phone registered the incoming call, I saw "DCS" and froze. Department of Child Services. Adam was now a court case, so a different division was assigned. They held all our lives in their hands as they ran through legal repose to the news that we were approved. With a gasp, I dropped the phone for an instant and asked them what to do next.

We met at the office we had been to before that smelled of old oceans of tears—the family meeting room of child protective services. The Department of Child Services had assigned a caseworker, and an advocate was there. You could feel the emotions of thousands of lost dreams. I hated that space for being so similar to the dark dungeon of the Neonatal Abstinence Syndrome room in the hospital.

We signed all the papers, but there was a catch. "It says here you have a disabled daughter?" The caseworker inquired. My heart sank as I realized this was the determining factor that could keep us from bringing home that innocent child. I couldn't believe that they hadn't mentioned this earlier. I was brought to tears in an instant. They asked for her diagnosis as I had been vague on the reports and only said mentally disabled.

As I softly said schizophrenia, I saw that same fear as the naive public on their faces, and I prepared for the worst. The CPS director was called in, and they had a consultation in the other room. I don't think I breathed the entire time they were gone. I just looked at my helpless life partner. My husband was shaking, and I was in shock. We reached out for each other's hands.

As they entered the room, their faces could not be read. They motioned for the caseworker to come over, handed her a paper, and asked her to make a copy. As they gave us the next thing to sign, it read; Will not allow and never alone. I breathed a huge sigh. They explained they had to be protective of Adam. We weren't allowed to let my mentally disabled daughter be with him alone or hold him unsupervised. Well, duh, was all I could think.

Once home, my husband and I sat out in our backyard oasis. Blankly, we stared at each other, then back to the pool. A large fence had been required to be installed, and I hated the interruption of the view. It was worth it for the safety and requirements of foster, but I didn't have to like it. Peering into the depths of the soothing water, we both seemed in shock. We hadn't expected to become parents at this time in our lives. He was sixty-one, and I was fifty-three. His youngest child was twelve. Mine was twenty-three. Now we were relative foster to an innocent baby boy.

"Congratulations!" We both said at once, nervously laughing.

"What's your schedule tomorrow?" I gazed at my husband. Someone had to actually pick Adam up from the hospital, and we were both scheduled to work. "I have personal leave time I can take." I offered. It was settled. He would go to work, as usual. I would pick up our sweet little man.

"I'm getting in the car to go pick him up." I phoned Elyse. My daughter was devastated at the news but knew what she had done. She desperately wanted to get better. The demon world of drugs had its lure secured tightly, and she fought it every day.

"Call me when you get home, kiss my sweet boy and tell him mommy loves him." I could hear her tears as she hung up.

"Damn it," I uttered as I wrestled the car seat base into place.

I had a baby? I rehearsed what to say to human resources. Luckily, I had known the lady there for years, and she was so sweet. "Congratulations! How awesome." and she marked down the personal leave day.

Already yawning from not sleeping well, I tapped on the steering wheel and switched the radio back and forth, searching for anything soothing. It felt like a movie unfolding before me. A drug addict, a schizophrenic, two wonderful stepchildren, five dogs, my wonderful husband, and partridge in a pear tree? (which is me)... and now an innocent little baby boy.

You have to follow special hospital pick-up rules when you're a foster. Switching off the radio, I noticed I was trembling. This was happening! I read the instructions intently. I wanted to make sure I followed their rules, and there were so many to master: Nothing in the bed with them, must have formula, clean bottles, etc. Your caseworker will randomly show up at your house. At least once a month, they will do a report.

February 23rd, 2017, after seven weeks in the NICU, I drove to the hospital to pick up our little miracle. The social worker had him in the car seat I provided, and they were required to watch while I buckled it in the backseat. I was grateful I had practiced a few times, and I felt like a student being graded for school. I passed the exam and was handed a signed note, and she asked me for my driver's license.

She did all her required life-altering signatures and reached out to shake my hand. I was startled by this, and I happily said. "Thank you for all that you do." I couldn't imagine the things these social workers go through.

Holding my hand too long, she said. "Thank you, not every infant here is as lucky as him." She smiled through her gapped teeth and glanced at Adam, all bundled up and smiling. "Good luck to you both."

I was so grateful for all the dedicated, overworked angels that saved this little child's life. I'm amazed by their abilities and the strength they share with all those so vulnerable. My gratitude would be genuinely unending.

Cautious and alone, I started my car and adjusted the child-safe mirror. We had installed it to see his little face while we drove. Together we meandered through the maze of the hospital parking garage. When we emerged on the street, I cautiously looked in both directions and back again. Anyone that has transported a baby out of a hospital garage for the first time knows it was a different kind of scary. Looking back at the mirror, his little eyes widened as they met mine. Inhale, exhale, breathe...I prayed aloud. "Lord, please guide me." Gazing for a moment at the miracle of this child, I assured this precious being. "It's going to be ok, little man." He smiled as big as the world, "I got you." I smiled back.

Chapter Twelve

FIRED

Joyful infant cries were ever-present as Adam was always hungry. He slept in spurts. I didn't mind the three am feedings. Blessed, I just felt blessed to hold him. I stared at that little face, those bright, innocent eyes. I was lost in their rivers of hope. Streaming tears had been frequent as I was ever reminded of the day I sat with him in that lonely and isolated place. I was simply happy to have him in my lap.

Ah, the smell of an infant child's head. They should bottle it up and sell it at the department store. I thought as I lay him down in his crib without blankets and no teddy bear. I was still under the critical eyes of the Department of Child Services' gaze. They looked at Adam's condition and went all around. The social worker showed up once a month, opened my fridge, checked his bed. She had a clipboard with boxes, and the checks were all made.

I was thankful the social worker didn't ask me about Marissa. She had been having more and more episodes, and I was grateful she had started using Uber to go to yet another friend's house. At least she wasn't home. There seemed to be nothing I could do to help her. Every night she would drink a half-gallon of juice. She said the medicine made her thirsty. And every morning, as my first chore, I would clean up her throw up from the bathroom floor. It was just my normal. Put the coffee pod in the Keurig, clean up the puke, wash hands, time for coffee.

I locked my bedroom door at night, where we kept Adam's crib. When my stepkids were over, I was glad they stayed in our beautifully finished basement. The downstairs bathroom was fit for a king with heated floors and a huge walk-in rain shower. They even had their own kitchen. It was a fabulous house. But it became a den of despair for the evil that happened in the other parts of that home. It was ample open space for those that would take advantage of an overworked mother who now had an infant.

Family court was the second hellish place I had been. Cold and uncaring with lives in the balance at every "all rise." It always smelled of people who smoke in their cars. The withdrawing addict twitched and scratched with chemicals of evil despair in their sweat. The smell permeated the air. It was a smell I knew well, and it triggered me. I flashed back to dirty socks thrown behind the bed. You could smell them from the other side of the house. Years of abuse that no one had known. Keeping those years buried inside until this smell brings them up in this harsh, cold courtroom.

I hated it there. Dockets always had a hundred people scheduled at the same time. But the judge was always late. We all jammed together as they were called one by one. I always had to take off work. How was anyone supposed to maintain a job and make it to all these five-hour-long hearings? They all seemed to never end. Everyone was on edge and making some kind of nervous gesture. Babies of all ages with unseen faces, their lives in the balance of every judge's decision. One by one, their horrible stories were flung out in the open for all to hear. It mainly was a pit of despair. Several times you heard a thump, and a person had fallen to the floor. Asleep or just bored or passed out from withdrawal. When they finally called our case, it was always very short and continued.

After eight long months, in October 2017, my cherished Elyse did something that made me the proudest I'd ever been. She agreed to sign her rights over to us and allowed us to become Adam's legal guardians. The judge signed the agreement as we stood hand and hand. Me, Elyse, and my wonderful husband; together, we would parent this innocent child. My daughter's decision to put her son's needs ahead of her own gave me hope that someday she would be free of her demons.

Marissa had become increasingly unstable. I did what I could to help her manage her symptoms. She loved Adam. She would make funny faces at him, and he would laugh. I so wanted her to be "normal." I wondered what it would be like to see her at college graduation. Her sparkling eyes and gleeful smile.

When meeting my childhood friends, I always tried to sway from the "what about Marissa?" I practiced saying, "oh, she's fine." It's not like anyone wants to hear. Well, she's been in a mental hospital twenty times since 2012. Her version of a good day is not feeling a thousand people raping her or puking uncontrollably. I listen to my classmates complain about tuition and their child not getting the best grades or a DUI. I wanted to scream at them to be grateful! I had a daughter that was ninety pounds at five feet, seven inches. She can't stay away from the demon fentanyl and lives in her car. Oh, and a daughter that sometimes doesn't know her name or what day it is and thinks she is two or sixteen, that hears "voices" twenty-four hours a day, seven days a week, and people raping her. Oh, and I had a baby?

I wished it was funny, but it wasn't. It was a harsh reality. Day in and day out, I managed my horrible job. I was one of the highest-paid for my position because I'd been there so long, and they were trying to get me to quit. Pressured, I needed an escape from this hole and prison of a job and focus on Adam. He was cognitively behind and had been receiving extra care with physical therapy. At eight months old, he passed the threshold and was released from the special needs program. He thrived at daycare, and they were taken by his larger-than-life personality.

"He's all boy, all the time." His daycare worker would say.

We made a plan and bought some land. We were moving to the country. Away from the drugs, away from everything. A peaceful place to raise an innocent child. A place where we could build our future-focused on Adam. We drew up the plans and started the process. I had to stay at my job until the construction loan was closed.

Then on Thursday, March 15th, 2018, Adam was fourteen months old. I was instant messaging a salesman at our company. I asked what our boss was doing since his chat bubble said he was out of the office. I wrote on the chat, "maybe he's coming here to fire me." I knew something was up since they were reorganizing the company again, and they didn't include me in the meetings.

I just put my head down and did my best. When I saw my boss and a lady from HR pull up, I wasn't surprised at all. I had a branch office; our headquarters was in Wisconsin. They had flown to Louisville just to fire me. I had been with the company for nineteen years and three months. Almost twenty years of loyal service. They waltzed in at ten am, handed me a severance package with a gag order, and asked for my keys.

I was distraught that they also fired the lady that worked with me. She hadn't liked the new plan either, but we both were the breadwinners that supported our families. I typed on the instant message still open on my screen." I was right. It was nice working with you," and closed the chat and went to sign the documents. I was horribly relieved and shocked, and scared all at once. Our timeline for moving just got moved up! We weren't going to be able to afford our oasis backyard house.

Schizophrenics don't handle change well. It was difficult for Marissa to transition to the fabulous house even though she had the room that overlooked the pool. It didn't matter to her; she just didn't like change. I knew I needed to warn her we would be moving again. After getting fired, I went home to let it sink in. Marissa was in her room, so I knocked and went in to give her the regular lunchtime meds. Her arm was out of the covers, and I noticed some marks on her arms. It was tiny dots all in a row. No, please tell me those aren't needle marks.

But it was. My heart broke that sad day when I came to realize the demon had come back into my precious middle child's life. I fell to the floor of her room. *No, please, no.* The carpet was matted with coffee, food, and nail polish. The utter devastation of hopelessness returned. I left as I watched her sleeping. *What was I going to do now?* As I got in my car to just drive around, my phone rang.

The daycare worker said, "Adam's got a fever."

"I'm on my way." When I arrived, my sweet little man was all red-faced and pale. I picked him up, and he clung to me. Cuddling my shoulder, his damp hair brushed my chin. At that moment, I knew that I had to choose. My schizophrenic daughter or my infant son. I would not allow a drug addict in my home, no matter the underlying circumstance. I needed a plan. I held him tightly as I stood in the parking lot of the daycare. I needed to be sure he was alright before strapping him backward into the car seat. Even though he obviously wasn't feeling well, Adam smiled as vast as the ocean.

Friday morning, I put the pod in the Keurig, cleaned up the puke, and washed my hands. After finishing my coffee, I got Adam dressed and took him to daycare. It was time to face Marissa. Standing at her door, I wanted to cry, hug, and slap her. How could she go back to this demon, I thought. But, I don't know how I would handle the torturous life she led day after day. No excuses, No excuses! I knocked on the door. She wasn't awake, and I came to her side.

I woke her gently and gave her my coffee. "We have to talk." She opened her once sparkling eyes.

"What's up? "She said nonchalantly.

"I saw your arm when I came to wake you yesterday."

"You what?" She ranted about me not knowing what I was talking about and blah, blah, witch, Magicland, the line, the line.

"Rehab or out– now! Pack your bag, and I'll take you. Or Uber can take you and your things somewhere else. Drug addicts aren't welcome in our home. Period!"

I heard through Elyse that she ended up at Sean's house. It was peaceful in the house for a few days. House prep had to get done, the real estate ads had to be placed, and the house had to be packed. The first person to look at our home bought it for full asking without a realtor. I didn't even put a sign in the yard.

Sean had been picked up on a warrant, so Marissa wanted to come home. I said, "rehab or no." And the twenty-second time to the hospital it was. They knew her already, and I left after the staff took her from the lobby. I didn't want to go to the intake this time. I just had enough of that room. I hoped that this time, things would be different.

I stared at the iPad she used to watch Netflix. "I need a boy-girl now." These were instant messages lining up drug deals. I took a long draw-in. Packed up the altar she had made to the Goddess of Magicland. Carefully, I labeled each box. I threw all her clothes from the floor in the washer. I carefully went through each pocket. Putting on gloves to go through her drawers, I packed up the sad remnants of her tormented life. We put our beautiful home contents into storage and made a special area marked "Marissa's stuff." Her illness was not kind when it came to change, and I knew she would have episodes. At that moment, I wanted answers. What do you do when they can't live with you? Is there a group home, a halfway house, or a facility where Marissa could live if she was too unstable to stay with us?

Naomi, my beloved eldest daughter, had let us stay in her walk-out basement until our new house in the country was finished. When I picked Marissa up from the rehab, she was herself again. I hugged her like a mom who embraces a lost child. Her face was full, and her eyes sparkled again. She looked excited to get home to her room. I repeatedly explained that we had to move, but she didn't seem to understand.

Marissa reluctantly went into this cold environment and settled into her bed. She asked, "where's my stuff?" I took her to get what could fit in her bag, and she talked to herself on the way. I saw her hand gestures, and her eyes went to the place where her illness took the stage. "I want my own place; help me get my own place." She had a friend that lived in the housing authority apartments, and she wanted to live there.

The next day I took her and filled out the housing authority paperwork. "There's a waiting list." Is all they said.

I took her to her endless dr appointments and rehab. Nothing took away her symptoms, and it was hard to live in such close quarters with Adam between my husband and me and Marissa in her room. We could hear every word, and there was only one bathroom. It was damp and dark and cold.

I tried to bring joy with music, happy television, and cartoons. We had many joyful moments with Naomi and her fiancé, who had returned with my granddaughter from California. Some of my life was a miraculous melody. I had never been free of the daily grind of horrible work life. I felt lost and found at the same time. I took Adam in his stroller on walks around the neighborhood. The wonder in his eyes while he watched trees and birds. Being fired had freed me and allowed me to celebrate the good.

Chapter Thirteen

FOREVER

"Housing Authority" registered on my incoming calls, and I prayed. August is scorching in Southern Indiana, so we all spent most days inside. It was 2018. Marissa had asked me about her own apartment every day for two months. She had episode after episode in that tiny room in Naomi's basement. I hoped this would be the change Marissa needed.

"An apartment has become available." The kind lady's voice sounded surprised.

With pensive optimism, my husband and I loaded Marissa's stuff from her section at storage. I found a table and chairs that had been in my office. A couch from a thrift store, our old tv, a desk, lamp. She was good to go. As she talked to the "voices" and hands moved to the orbs, we skipped through the grocery parking lot once more. These groceries would be unpacked inside her shelves and drawers.

When we left that evening, I reminded her to lock her door. I laid my hand on the house number. *Lord, please protect her.* My precious, horribly mentally ill, beautiful blue-eyed Marissa was alone in public housing. Is this the best I could do? I tried to think of another route, a different possibility. *Please Lord, let her be ok,* I thought to myself.

The season had changed; Fall's majesty had begun. My mom's instinct, high alert, had been triggered again. Her apartment smelled like a jail cell must smell after a drunk had thrown up there for a week. I went there several times a week to give her meds and get her groceries. By the second month, her neighbor was out, and she pulled me aside.

"What's going on with her? That poor child screams every night for hours." She explained that the other neighbor below her had filed a complaint about it. She told me the police had been called twice in the last week. Panic set in as I had noticed Marissa drifting further and further into her schizophrenic-induced hole of blackness. She had become increasingly distant and unaware, and it was a different feeling—a dark, ominous, looming sense.

As I woke one morning to the shining bright eyes of my sweet baby boy, something felt different. Mother's intuition remained on high alert but now had shadowy figures to go along with it. I got up and looked all around. I went upstairs to see if anyone was there. It was just Adam and I and the dogs. Evil, I just couldn't shake the uneasiness. I had arranged for my mother to watch Adam for a few hours as I had to take Marissa to get her prescriptions. The smell of cinnamon and nutmeg and vanilla warmed my soul as we entered my mother's house. She was good at making us welcome.

The closer I got to Marissa's tiny apartment, the more the uneasiness grew. As I passed the car with the broken window, I was startled by the black garbage bag attempting to keep out the rain. The blackness slapped the air. The crisp fall breeze was no match to the heaviness on my mind. As I pulled into the parking lot, I started to text, but she was already hanging on the curb. Her cigarette hung half out of her mouth. With a staggering gait, she walked to my car and got in. But the standard "what's up" was gone.

"Hey, how's it going?" I heard myself say as I tried to turn off the fear.

Chills overtook the crisp fall air and crept up my spine. I tried to exhale, and my breath just stayed there like someone had taken it away. She looked me straight in the eye, but she wasn't there. The evil one had emerged even darker than before, she paused, staring straight at my soul.

"One day, I'm going to kill you, and it will be forever." Her voice was sinister as she suddenly looked away.

I froze, and my instinct to bolt out the door was overcome by my concern. "What?" Even though her words pierced through my brain in an etching that would never leave.

She made the most devilish laugh and said. "Are we going? Let's go."

It was the longest five-minute drive of my life. Marissa burst out screaming at the pharmacy window that she was the white witch, she was in charge, and I didn't understand. She said she could kill people and bring them back. "Boop, like that. See, cut off their heads and then boop, just like that."

Boop? I gasped. I got her antipsychotic and gave her the dose before moving out of the lane. I drove the five minutes back to her apartment, and she arrogantly got out of the car. Without turning around, Marissa went back to the curb with her lighter and lit her cigarette. Flipping her hand backward, she dismissed me as if she was a queen dismissing her court.

As I drove past that car with the flapping black whip, her words echoed. I thought for a moment. *Maybe that was a dream?* I wished that it had been. Tears of what may come next played a tragic role in my head. *What was I supposed to do?* I sat crying in the Target parking lot for an hour, just processing the words that my precious middle daughter had just said.

I gathered myself and picked up Adam and fake-smiled, ate pie, and laughed. My mother did not know what had just transpired, and I hugged my sweet boy.

"I love you, my sweet boy. Thanks for watching him, Mom." I leaned into my mother for comfort. She never knew why. She probably felt it but knew not to ask.

Elyse was one of those kids that is not afraid of anything. When she woke me at two am with terror in her voice, my mom's intuition was again on high alert.

"Marissa tried to kill me with scissors! She came after Sean with a hammer. We got out of there. She told everyone to go and was talking about death. All this stuff about death. Mom, you have to do something." I bolted out of bed.

My mind went back to my earlier days of her and the diagram I'd found in her room. The time she called me while walking in the rain on the highway. She was no stranger to the enticement of suicide. I had no idea what to do.

The "One day I'm going to kill you all the way, and it will be forever" echoed in my mind. She wanted to kill me because these personalities saw me as a threat. I was trying to get them to leave. This is common among schizophrenics whose minds trick them into thinking their caregivers are the enemy.

As I heard myself try to explain to the police, the dark cloud of despair hung overhead. I listened to the officer recommend a welfare check. They must have had to get me to say, "will you please do a welfare check?" Because they kept asking me that question over and over.

"Do you want us to do a welfare check? So, you want us to do a welfare check?" Yes! I want you to help her. And obviously, check to make sure she's not trying to kill herself (or anyone else). Since it's the weekend, there was no way to get an Emergency Detention Order so they could put her in holding for her own safety. Those had to be recommended by a physiatrist, and the order had to be signed by a judge. It was a process I knew all too well.

Looking back, I should have gone there myself. I don't know how that would have gone, but I sure wish I could find out. I called the police back after a few hours. Worrying was not a strong enough word. After it was released, I read the police report: We approached the door and knocked and identified ourselves as police. The subject opened the door and saw us. The subject ran up the stairs screaming about a witch and a demon. The subject then proceeded to run back down the stairs and attacked the officer screaming about him being a demon. After knocking the officer to the ground, the subject ran into the parking lot. We pursued and knocked the subject to the ground.

Lightheaded from not breathing, I fell to my knees and prayed. *Dear Lord, please help her.* "Assaulting a public safety officer causing moderate bodily injury, forcibly resisting arrest." I read her charges. My heart sank. A person having a psychotic episode has some kind of super-strength. One should never try to overpower them. But, they need hospitals, not jails.

My disabled, schizophrenic, chronically ill, sweet little girl Marissa was in jail. I had forgotten that antipsychotic medications started losing their effectiveness after six years or so. Her medications weren't helping her, and again she had turned to self-medication. This time she tried meth. I read that this drug is horrible for anyone with an underlying mental condition. That was a gross understatement when it came to Marissa. That was November 18th, 2018.

Chapter Fourteen

JAIL

Scream, all she did was scream. When her natural voice gave out, her internal voice screamed as the demons raged a silent war. One that was real to her. A thousand people raping me over and over, my thoughts echoed her words. They put her in the "booking area" of the jail. I called, and they refused to talk to me. I persistently called again and again and again. They didn't care that I had power of attorney.

No one cared. To them, I was just another hysterical mother. They finally gave me the name of the female inmate counselor. "I'm sorry we get a lot of those types here." She said,

What types are those? I thought to myself.

"My daughter Marissa is disabled with schizophrenia. She needs to be in the hospital." I tried to explain how she couldn't be without her medications. She's disabled; she has rights. She has to take her required medications. I insisted on talking to the staff that administers medication. They received me with the same "uh-huh" of the counselor and jail personnel. No one knew how to have her sent to the hospital for a proper evaluation and stronger medication. With an exhale, I marked off the twentieth person I had called in a row.

"We don't do that." I heard it over and over. No one cared. If they did, they didn't know how to help. I heard "there's a gap" in the care of these mentally ill inmates. "A gap" that was keeping a disabled schizophrenic that just had a major psychotic episode behind bars.

My resolve to fix this grew stronger and stronger, and I pleaded with the clerks and the judge. I wrote a long letter to the judge and sent it through the clerk. A recount of the years struggling to get to this point. An account of the disability that plagued Marissa's brain. She should get rights for this horrible and tragic disease that caused her to act this way. She needs medical attention, and she needs it now! No one did anything while my mentally disabled daughter sat in the booking area cell. No one did anything while she heard "voices" and saw demons and felt a thousand people raping her over and over. All she could do was scream.

All that mattered to them was the fact that she attacked an officer. Exhausted and repulsed by the lack of concern, I laid down to try and rest. Visions of her and her state made it nearly impossible to sleep. Snoring husband, cuddled up toddler, dogs vying for space, time for precious sleep. I watched as the clock ticked the hours away. Relieved when the alarm went off, it was time to face another day.

Sally was the counselor that had a good heart. She listened and met with my sweet Marissa. "She didn't make much sense," was all she could tell me. Marissa was fading away. "They're keeping her in booking because of her screaming. They're not allowing her in the general population. They put her in isolation for a few days to see if that would make her stop."

I was so upset. "They never stopped to consider that she had no control over the reactions?" I asked.

"I'm so sorry. I wish there was more I could do." She muttered as she hung up.

Who could I call? What could I do? No one cared. "She attacked a police officer" was said over and over. The medical staff at the jail prescribed her some sedatives and an antidepressant. They don't give antipsychotics in jail. "Budget doesn't allow it." They replied to my ever questioning of why. I found some who genuinely wanted to help. Mostly ones with mentally ill loved ones. But they came up blank when thinking of a solution. She remained in the booking area until her court date.

Marissa's hair, tangled and matted, hung at each side of her head as she shuffled with the orange plastic sandals they give inmates. Her hands cuffed behind her back. Clanking chains that were attached to each ankle echoed through the room. "All rise," the bailiff called. I fought back the tears. Was I really here watching my precious middle child shuffle down this courtroom aisle? Her stained jumpsuit overwhelmed the tiny outline of a person. This was my disabled, schizophrenic, freckled-faced, blue-eyed little girl.

I had to stop thinking as the gavel pounded. You could hear the weight of the creaking benches as that room full of heaviness sat. For over an hour, one after another, the stories of hell were told. The charges, the pleading, the forced silence among the accused's mothers and daughters and fathers and sons and children.

For twenty-nine long days, she'd been in this place. No antipsychotics had been prescribed. Only sedatives and antidepressants, no matter how many times I had begged. She hadn't received her required once-a-month shot. "If she ever goes off it, her mind will decompress," played over and over in my thoughts. Marissa agreed to plead guilty to the lesser charge of resisting, time served, and probation. "Do you understand these charges?" The judge asked her as she nodded and mumbled

"Uh, ok," Marissa mumbled.

As she shuffled back to her seat in the back, she saw me. Her face contorted as she attempted a freckle-faced smile. Her eyes told the story of the bewildered resentment of a mind that refused to comply. Her sentence was sixty days, but they gave her time served. The creaking bench loudly announced every grief-ridden shrug. Rain overhead only deepened the dark cloud that followed me out the door. Wiping the tears that had been building for hours, I sat in my car and wondered, *what's next?* I had to go pick up Adam. Taking charge of my conscience, I picked up my phone and went back to the business of life.

"DOC," Department of Corrections registered as my last ten missed calls. Flags on the courthouse whipped in the breeze as I saw Marissa standing on the sidewalk. Those orange flip-flops were better than bare feet on the cold pavement. A stranger's phone was in her hand that she handed back as she saw me and ran to me. Removing my jacket, I threw it over her shoulders as she started to whimper.

She trembled and muttered and managed, "Hi, mom." She melted into me as if she were an infant, and I couldn't stop the tears. Her clothes were the ones she had slept in for days those long twenty-nine days ago. Tie-dyed once-white tee shirt, tattered and stained, gray sweats three sizes too big held up with the string in the front.

Confused and disoriented, she asked where she was going. "Back to your apartment, I guess?" Is all I could say.

"Can we stop and get cigarettes? I really need cigarettes and a lighter, yeah, a lighter." I stopped at the gas station on the way, and she sat on the curb. Dinging bells on the door to the gas station rang as I purchased a lighter and Camel Turkish gold. She looked at these presents as if they were the best things in life as she puffed away like it was Christmas morning. For an hour, she sat there smoking one cigarette after another.

This was not the time to talk about the eviction she was facing. Inhaling her cheeseburger with only ketchup, she again started the dialogue with the "voices." She said she was in charge of the police on her block. That's how she survived in that hole.

With her arms flying in all directions, she said, "let me go," and we headed to where she was home. I didn't go up since I'd been there all morning, ensuring it was safe and secure. Her bedsheets and clothes had been washed, dried, and folded, and put away in the dresser of her youth. Milk, juice, e-cigarettes had been unpacked. The stains of what looked like a thousand nights of puking were cleaned up from her bathroom floor.

Whipping the car door open, she left without glancing, and I heard her say, "thanks, mom," at her door.

Marissa was back at that apartment without her medication. I saw the release papers on the seat where she had been. A prescription and a sheet of cardboard with the meds for the rest of the week. A document that read probation, along with a number to call. I knocked on Marissa's door, but she didn't answer, so I called. She had probably just laid down, so I drove to the pharmacy.

They said, "fifteen minutes," so I just waited.

Naomi was babysitting Adam, and my mind drifted to his mother, Elyse. I missed her so badly. I looked around the parking lot for her car. She lived with her boyfriend in a Buick skylark or couch hopped from one friend to another. My mind drifted to my ex, their father.

My ex had decided to help Marissa, and I was so relieved. *Maybe he will reach her where I couldn't,* is the lie I told myself. I secretly didn't know what else to do or where to turn. He had a way of getting what he wanted, and I was so hopeful this skill would help Marissa.

Pulling up to her apartment, self-pity-party behind me, I scanned the neighborhood. It's not the worst part of town, but it's close. I knew to be conscious of my surroundings. The white-haired lady stared at the street sign each day at precisely six o'clock. The man with the shiny "A" necklace always gave me a nod. The little girl on the curb, twirling her locks and playing with her Ken doll. All looked secure, and I headed up to knock.

After a few minutes, I tried to call, but it went straight to voicemail. I shouted and pounded and went back to my car. I sat there and smiled at the little girl and wondered what to do. Just as I put my hand on the ignition, my phone rang.

"Mom, did you call me?" Marissa asked. When she opened the door, I gave her the meds and a bottle of water and watched her gulp the night's dose without hesitation. "Ok," Marissa dismissed me with her hand, and without another word, slammed the door in my face. I heard her scream something once she was inside, and I turned to return to my car.

A close presence startled me, and I jumped. It was Elyse! I hadn't seen her in several weeks. Tears streamed down my face as I hugged her, and she told me she'd been staying at Marissa's apartment taking care of the birds. I asked her if she had somewhere else to sleep, and she shrugged as she always did. We hugged like mother's and daughter's do, and she turned to her friend.

I gave Elyse my sandwich and some water, and whatever food I had in my car. "I love you no matter what," is all I could mutter.

"I knew you'd been here." She said I guess she had come and realized Marissa must be getting out of jail because of the cleaning. Our conversations were always strained and guarded, but there was never a question of our love. She asked about Adam, and I told an antic from that day or the day before. She smiled behind her tears, and our eyes met, and we both quickly turned away.

"I'll call you later." Elyse's voice echoed in the parking lot as she got into her friend's rusty car. As I watched them drive off, I realized that this day was a blessing. I had the precious, rare privilege to hug each of my biological daughters.

Chapter Fifteen

MERRY CHRISTMAS, I QUIT

My Ex was in charge now; I gave him the info with all Marissa's doctors and where this gets filled, and all the required probation and numbers. I was so relieved. I felt like a weight had finally been lifted, and maybe I could go back to my life. With my loving husband and wonderful step kids, and sweet little Adam. As Marissa's payee, I still had to do all that paperwork and give her the money when asked. She continued to stray from her prescribed medications.

On Christmas, it'd been a week since Marissa and I had spoken. With her presents in my lap, I parked by her apartment. I knew the time by the lady staring at the street sign, six o'clock on the dot. I checked my surroundings. Pulling my scarf tightly, I walked up to her door and exhaled as I knocked… and waited… and knocked… and waiting. No sounds from inside, and no one was around.

With my hand on her door, I prayed in a whisper, "Please Lord, let her be ok." I wrote her a note and attached it with the scotch tape I had in my car from wrapping her presents. It read: Merry Christmas, my daughter. I love you no matter what.

It was another week before I heard, "Hey mom, what's up?" I wanted to slap her and hug her. The heartbreak of not hearing or seeing her on Christmas was a worrying mother's nightmare. "I need my money, like all of it," was her demonic insistence. Still trembling at the evil voice that had returned with a vengeance, I hung up the phone.

A few minutes later, my phone registered a blocked number I answered. "Are you Marissa Mark's mother?" The officer inquired. I went into the two hundredth explanation of my daughter's hallucinations. By now, they all knew her but had to follow the rules and make the call.

The "like all of it" conversation with the evil persona hovered over me. "Forever" is a word I heard in my nightmares, and those piercing eyes that weren't my child haunted me. Tears I'd contained for another month of frustration hit me all at once.

As I handed the twenty out of the window, I told my schizophrenic daughter, "I decided to quit as your payee."

"That's cool. I want my money. It's cool." She shakily replied.

"You'll have to assign someone else," I warned her. I drove out of the parking lot while the little girl on the curb smiled at me. The garbage bag whipped, but this time I wasn't startled as I drove past the car with the broken window for the last time.

The Social Security Administration door was so cold as I pushed it open on that January morning. With a two-year-old toddler in tow, I took my required number and sat on the floor with a thousand others. Social security was flooded with faces of different races, and I heard Spanish and English simultaneously. My terrible two toddlers did not like to stay still, and he kept trying to run all around. He was so determined that several people in line gave me pity and tried to help out. Peek a boo, I see you. Launched a man with one eye, and I thought about the irony of that. You find such sweet people in these places where misery lives next to married name changes and students just trying to get their social security cards.

The kindness of others humbled me to the reality that we all have our stories to tell. It always surprised me that the troubled ones never hesitated to offer to help when in public. I guess they were tuned in to the fact that I was clueless and genuinely stuck. I would learn even more later about these kind people and their helpfulness.

"I want to quit being a payee." I heard myself mumble as I struggled to hold my sweet little boy. He wrestled and wrangled and pulled my hair and screamed. The worker behind her glass counter offered Adam a sucker. He took it and flung it and hit an old lady in the head.

"Sign here and here, you know she'll lose her benefits until someone else gets assigned?" She asked.

"I warned her, thanks." I handed the paperwork back.

The lady pity smiled at me. "You're all set."

The pity smile...my mind drifted off for a moment. A smile I knew well from the times at the store while I tried to check out with my daughter in tow. Marissa would glare all-around at the orbs and the angels and talk to dead people aloud. Frozen air caught me off guard as I left the building, or maybe it was the reality of what I'd just done.

Strapped in his car seat and thoroughly exhausted, I watched Adam drift off. My thoughts wandered to Marissa, and the sadness hit me. I just wanted my daughter back. I sat with the paperwork flung in the front seat. I watched the innocence of this toddler through the tears of my lost daughter while it started to snow. *What's next?* I wondered. Stop feeling sorry for yourself and make a plan.

I had created an email for exchanges of data with my ex regarding Marissa. In the few weeks that followed, she was evicted from her apartment. Her dad had the reins, and I tried to stay away and focused on programs or housing available to her. I was told. "We don't have a program that fits her needs." "You have to have a cognitive disability to qualify." And "We could help if she had private insurance." And "She would have to comply with regular drug screens."

I heard, "there's a gap." Followed by "call the media" and "call your representative." There was always a reason that wasn't a reason.

Her probation officer suggested Adult Protective Services. I heard, "try adult guardianship." I called them all. I was desperate to find her a home. My ex sent me messages through a special email about all the calls he had made. One day he wrote, "I had no idea," and I could tell he was genuinely concerned by the severity of her illness.

Another trip to the mental hospital and another visit later, and it just seemed to go on and on—episode after episode. My Ex and his fiancé eventually had to make her leave their apartment.

Marissa had no place to go. "Mom, can I stay there?"

I paused and then said, "No, that's not an option." My daughter was homeless and schizophrenic with nowhere to go. People would call me with sightings of her. "She was sleeping behind the liquor store off Market. "Or, "I saw her at the side of Starbucks, and I bought her some coffee." Her sightings were comforting and terrifying as I wanted to hug her and help her. But, Marissa was off her medication, and the evil was too unpredictable.

In December 2018, I had heard she was staying with the stepfather of one of her "friends." I saw where she'd missed a court date, and I waited for the warrant to come up online. I called the police, and I told them where she was staying. I hit the refresh button over and over on the case summary to see if she had been found. The jail was so much safer and might give me the time to find someone to help her.

My Ex was also searching and pleading for programs or homes or hospitals to house her. No one could be found. Marissa didn't qualify for anything except treatment for her psychosis. Sadly, the reality was that there was no cure, and stabilization was just a band-aid to her long-term needs. She had no access to the drugs she took for the symptoms she couldn't control. What are we supposed to do? She's too unstable to live with either family that loves her. At least she's in jail now and not sleeping on a bench or a porch that she calls "her living room."

Visions of Marissa in that cell once again took center stage. "DOC" on my missed calls was a code she needed money to buy Little Debbie's and e-cigarettes. Again, I sent the letter to the judge, and I pleaded. "Please don't let her out, she has nowhere to go, and I'm trying to work something out." She's been in the hospital so many times. Vanilla and cinnamon filled the air as I cooked my special pancakes for my wonderful family, trying to bring the good out. At the same time, I dealt with this desperate situation.

I worked with a liaison between the jail and the state hospital. I spent several months sending emails and calling and gathering the three hundred pages of medical records to prove she was "in need of services." In the jail where she was, they don't do counseling or give services unless the inmate requests. A person that thinks there in charge of the demons and talks to dead people and witches and feels people raping her. Arrogantly, Marissa sat there controlling the orbs so they'd come for your soul. All she wanted was more drugs. Convinced that was the answer, not talking to some chic about what it was like to be her. Again she was screaming and screaming for hours until her voice was silent.

After months, the liaison had the special committee look at Marissa's case. Marissa needed a recommendation to the state hospital where she could be transferred. They have group homes that are lifetime habitats. This was the best news and only hope that I'd heard in a year of trying to find shelter for her. I held my breath as her email came across. It's been too long since she has been "in services" to make the recommendation. I read it two times before it sunk in that since Marissa couldn't ask for help, it was deemed that it had been too long since she'd been "in services" to know whether she needed services. What the hell?

She spent several more months in that jail cell. I couldn't give up, and I worked with her probation officer. According to Google, "In the United States, Adult Protective Services(APS) are agencies that provide protective social services to elderly adults (typically those age 60 or 65 or older) as well as vulnerable adults (typically those with serious disabilities)." This was my daughter! She has had a serious disability for years! Of course, then I Googled the definition of serious disability. "A physical or mental impairment that substantially limits the major life activities of a patient." I'd say not being about to tell what is real is a serious impairment!

Twenty minutes into my conversation with the head of Adult Protective services, she said. "Most people take guardianship of their family members."

"No, she can't live with me. She threatened to kill me. I can't be responsible for an adult when I can't control their actions." I angrily replied.

"Oh, they don't have to live with you. You aren't responsible for their actions." She attempted. Lady, I called an attorney and paid to learn that it certainly does make me responsible for her actions if I take guardianship of her. I wanted to say.

"She thinks she can kill people and bring them back. She threatens to do this regularly. Isn't it Adult Protective Services' job to protect her since she is an adult with a serious mental impairment?" I said, trying to explain my frustration.

"Oh, we usually only help the elderly, and those people usually have guardians." She explained.

I realized there's nowhere for them to house anyone with Marissa's illness. She's too young for the state to take responsibility for her. She didn't have a cognitive diagnosis from birth or a physically disabling condition **and** a mental disability. Both were required to qualify for the long term care that she needed. **This was the gap everyone had been talking about.**

September, on her birthday, she had once again been released to the hard streets. I heard she had been spotted by a park and I walked all around looking for her. I had gotten her a gift card from Qdoba, and I was determined to find her. Her hair was a shade darker, but I knew my precious daughter as I glanced on the porch "living room." When she saw me, she looked past me as if I was transparent. Then her gaze came to rest when I got up beside her.

She didn't seem to know me until I said, "Happy birthday, Marissa."

Confused and disoriented, "it's my birthday?" She stammered. "Mom?" She hugged me, but no one was there. I'll never forget hugging that shell of a body with no feeling of anyone inside—a hollowed soul with no emotion or expression. Tears started dripping onto the dirty couch where she slept.

Quickly, I sat the gift card on the table by her ashtray that had overflowed. I ran to my car, and I didn't look back. My daughter was gone.

The next day on a warrant, she was picked up again. The stepfather from the porch where she'd been staying got my number from one of my spotters. He wanted me to get her stuff. I picked up the gift card still on the table and left with a tote I couldn't bear to open. Her lifetime of memories and pictures of old dreams in the pages. It was her tote from her life as a child. Before her illness, before all the "voices." A time when her light sparkled. The life she was

Chapter Sixteen

INCOMPETENT

$$\bullet\!\!\!\!\rightarrow\!\!\!\!\times\!\!\!\!\leftarrow\!\!\!\!\bullet$$

"Competency evaluation filed." I saw the words on the case summary. Daily, I had the site pulled up to see if any progress had been made. Her chance at real help was at the state hospital. I'd been calling the probation officer and talking to the inmate counselor. Marissa kept calling as I was her lifeline to Little Debbie's and more e-cigarettes. She would only speak for a minute and then usually drop the phone.

The counselor said Marissa was increasingly distant, and her erratic behavior had landed her in isolation. She violated probation and had another "resisting arrest" offense, so they weren't releasing her. I was so relieved. Marissa had been homeless for months. She'd gone to the local mental hospital; they'd stabilized her and released her to the street. She'd get picked up by the police for one charge or another. Sometimes just because her hysterical mother would find her and call them and remind them she was a person, and they'd keep her overnight.

When the sightings happened, I would go try to find her. With my gun tucked in the tank top holster and eyes darting all around. On my way to the grocery, I glanced at the bag in the back seat. Pillow, blanket, baby food, wipes, bottled waters, flashlight, just in case I found her. She called from the homeless shelter one day and asked me for coffee for her and her friend. She was too unstable to stay with me, but I still tried to ensure she had food and drinks.

She would beg me each time she saw me. "Please, mom, let me stay with you." But her behavior was too unstable, and my heart broke each time I had to tell her no. There was nothing and no one that seemed to find a solution to where she could get long-term care. At least she was safer than the street when she was in jail. I was relieved she was behind bars for now.

In October, I was on vacation in Florida. Because it was my son Adam's nap time, I stayed behind while the others went fishing. Looking into that innocent sleeping face, I checked Marissa's case summary on my phone. It had been a month since the competency evaluation was filed in court. Slowly, I scrolled down to read all the fine print in the case summary. Coming to the end of the long legal blah, blah, I finally got to the phrases. It took me a minute to absorb. I read it over and over. "Found lacking incapacity to stand trial." I read softly aloud once again. I closed my eyes and surrendered to the tears.

My precious Marissa was found incompetent. Now she could be transferred to the state hospital and get the desperately needed help.

The little boy sleeping in my lap opened his eyes. "What's the matter, momma?"

I smiled through my tears. "Momma's happy sweet boy, Auntie Marissa, is gonna be ok. She's going to have a safe place to live."

Back at home, I kept checking the case file and calling the jail for updates. "My daughter was found incompetent. Why is she there?" My voice was too loud to be heard. Usually, I was able to keep calm when dealing with people who'd like nothing better than to hang up on me.

"There's no bed available at the State hospital." They explained. My beautiful, precious, schizophrenic daughter was still screaming and tortured in the tiny isolation room a month after the "lack of capacity" ruling. She still sat in jail.

They couldn't order the transport to the State hospital until a bed was released. Waiting on hold for the second state hospital, I pleaded with admissions and told them the story.

"I'm sorry, there's an epidemic of mental illness. We just don't have enough beds," was the answer I got at all three state hospitals. "You should go to the media." And "call your representative." And, "get in a support group."' And, of course, "there's a gap." I heard all these phrases again as I desperately called to find a bed for my disabled, schizophrenic daughter.

It wasn't her fault that she had this diagnosis instead of a lost limb or brain cancer, spina bifida, or autism. These diagnoses carry excellent solutions, and health care providers are abundantly available.

Schizophrenia was an illness no one wanted to deal with. Skipped by society and politicians long ago in tall buildings that looked down upon us all. It was a horrifying reality for us mothers, fathers, and brothers and sisters of those with schizophrenia. No longer able to get long-term commitments for those who need twenty-four hours a daycare.

At the time, I didn't know this, and I fought for my daughter to get into this haven where they care for schizophrenics as if they are real people that are loved. One month and one day after receiving the ruling with all my calling and pleading, my daughter was transported the three-hour drive to the state hospital. An entire month of waiting in a jail cell, after being found incompetent, for a hospital bed to become available.

Coming in from the simplicity of mowing my five acres, "Richmond State Hospital" registered on my missed calls. With the usual "I have POA" conservation, I emailed the document that allowed them to talk to me. Holding my breath, I redialed, and a voice said. "Can I help you?"

"I'll ask her to call you." Hanging up the phone, I could hear screaming and shouting in the background. I recognized the voice as if she was just born. It was Marissa asking for the phone.

Ten long minutes later, "Richmond State Hospital" showed again on my incoming call.

"Mom, I want to come home." Marissa whimpered.

"Please try to hang in there," was all I could whimper. "I love you no matter what."

I hung up on my daughter amidst her saying, "you said you'd always take care of me." It was a promise I was forced to break when she went down the dark hole of self-medication.

I mapped out the route to the state hospital, three hours one way. Reading the rules as I had packed the non-alcohol shampoo, conditioner, hairbrush, and comb. I bought brand new sweat outfits without the string ties, bobby pins, and tennis shoes without laces for playing in the courtyard. Three sets of pajamas with happy, bright-colored expressions, all packed neatly in a new suitcase for Marissa. I was going to see my little girl.

It was comforting to have my oldest daughter Naomi beside me as we slowly drove through the pouring rain. The radio was no distraction from the unending "mom, please." As much as I wanted to see Marissa, I dreaded the pleading, and I hoped she was well-medicated. When I read the visitation rules, I noticed we could bring food in for the patient and had taken Marissa's order. At Qdoba, we got the chicken queso burrito, white rice, no beans, two ladles of extra hot sauce in a bowl with the burrito on the side. At Starbucks, we got her white mocha latte.

Excitement and dread overcame me as we pulled into the parking lot. The building reminded me of my elementary gymnasium all those years ago. As we scanned for the right door, we noticed another family entering with food. We followed them, relieved to not have tried the wrong door, and set off the alarm. Mental hospitals all have different rules. Most don't allow cell phones or anything that can record or take pictures. We tried to think of things that wouldn't be allowed in the long line since they search you and every single thing you bring. If you have complicated items with you, it will take forever, and everyone else in line will be pissed.

Pizza boxes were opened, bags of chips were examined. Security pointed out the mirrored lid on the eyeshadow. Whoops! It took us a few minutes to pry out the mirror, and since we had broken the cover, we had to pry off the hinges as they were too sharp. Since we were newbies, they let us stand to the side while security scanned the others. The smell of a food court arose as all the different orders were checked.

The odor of disinfectant and dodge balls competed with the smell of the food as we entered. Sitting at a folding table with her legs crossed and fidgeting, I saw my precious Marissa. She shuffled in her orange flip-flops with her arms flying around.

With a genuine embrace, I notice her frail body. She melted into her mother, and I felt her... Tears streamed down my face as I attempted, "Hi, Marissa."

"Your hair is brown." Naomi managed as we sat across from each other.

"Yeah, I don't know what happened," Marissa said as she genuinely smiled.

The golden locks of her childhood were gone. She gobbled up her burrito and drank her now cold Starbucks like it was the first time she'd had either. Naomi carefully applied eyeshadow, eyeliner, and mascara. Marissa smiled at her sister, and her face was undistorted from the confusion that had plagued her so long. It's the first time in years that I'd seen them together. I flashed back to them like children playing in my makeup.

It was like the many times they played dress-up, power ranger, and hot lava. I thought of how they used to fight over who got to be the pink power ranger. I sat memorized by this rare moment when everything was harmonious and joyful. Most precious things are not things at all... they're moments in time that you have to recognize and appreciate.

In the mental hospital gymnasium, I watched as my children played dress-up. I felt peace and harmony. Marissa held up the new pj's laughing at the bright colored "need coffee" and the new sweat outfits she said were soooo cozy. Holding up her tennis shoes, she gleefully put them on, hopped up, and pranced around like a ballerina. Marissa hadn't had any shoes for months and was thrilled to have her own clothes to wear.

After about an hour and a half, I knew Marissa was weary of hiding her symptoms. It was a look that I knew very well. As we hugged for too long, I leaned over and kissed her forehead. So rare was the time when she was Marissa, and I lingered by her side.

"Mom, thank you so much for coming and all the new stuff. And oh, the burrito!"

Smiling, I blubbered, "I love you, my daughter. I'll be back in a few weeks."

As the door alarm buzzed and the door slammed behind us, I pulled myself together. Looking at Naomi, I saw the same look as my reflection.

"You ok?" I asked. She shrugged as security led us out.

Exhausted, we returned to Starbucks. Since our expectations were low, we agreed it went better than anticipated. Sometimes thinking the worst is our go-to defense mechanism. Naomi was no stranger to complicated situations. Naomi was the one who got the three am call that someone was in our yard and was going to kill and rape her. She's the one that got the call that Marissa was walking down the street with a garbage bag in the rain. In the early stages of Marissa's illness, Naomi found her sister on the side of the road. She persuaded her to sleep in her garage. Naomi pulled her back into the moving car on a winding road on a cliff. There was also her sister Elyse, her drug use, and her father.

As the snow started falling, my oldest leaned her head on my shoulder. "She looked so good," she whispered her thoughts about Marissa.

The windshield wipers waned back and forth as I fought back more tears. "Thanks for coming with me." I whimpered as I kissed her on the top of the head.

Naomi drifted off to sleep, and I paused to be thankful Marissa was alive. Grateful that she was Marissa today. She knew us and was glad to see us. Thankful for all the kind people who helped when I couldn't reach her. Grateful for the coffee that helped with the exhaustion from emotions.

Silently, I watched my first-born daughter Naomi sleep peacefully. My thoughts drifted to a time when my children were joyful and innocent. The snow reminded me of all those winter days with sledding and hot chocolate with marshmallows. Happy family times. Cherished memories of a time now lost. Lost to the seemingly endless road back home from the mental hospital.

As she got out of the car, Naomi and I embraced like two people who had just shared a rare moment. I paused in my garage as I transitioned to the Momma of a two-year-old toddler, wife, and stepmother. Grateful and humbled by the blessing of so many good things to celebrate.

Chapter Seventeen

NO WARNING

"Every two weeks, it was the same journey with different "orders." Rehab and hard work made it possible for my youngest daughter to come along for the Christmas visit. Sitting at the folding table with presents and pizza with jalapeno peppers, I caught myself drifting back to the past Christmas. Here she was right in front of me, safe and well cared for. I could hug her and not worry about "the evil." More tears came as I handed her the next present—a cozy Nightmare Before Christmas blanket, SpongeBob pajama pants, silly bright-colored toe socks.

I marveled at my youngest daughter Elyse. So brave and resilient. Addiction caught her every thought, and she was such a fighter. She now had some plump in her cheeks from ninety pounds a year ago. Adam was her motivation to keep striving to be a good role model. I always encouraged their ongoing relationship as long as she worked on herself. I drew a strict heavy line at what was allowed in our home. Most people wouldn't understand the gravity of what it was like to sit with these two daughters at the same time being "normal." We ate our cold pizza and drank our root beer, diet coke, and coffee with no care in the world.

We ended our visit early as Marissa was excited to have cookies and a party in her ward. Her face filled with laughter as I tripped on the blanket and tumbled to the floor. Both of their smiling faces are ingrained in my memory as each gave me their hand to pull me up. It was another rare memory as they helped their clumsy mother up off the floor. The security door alarm and our laughter echoed down the corridor as we parted. I watched Marissa walk away with her escort as the door slammed behind us.

We skipped to the car like we were in a movie, or maybe we were freezing from not having our coats. Whipping wind made driving uneasy. Celebrating the good, I paused to acknowledge and be grateful once more. Glancing over at baby Elyse, balled up like a puppy and snoring.

"Thanks for letting me come." She said as I dropped her off with some guy.

Lord, protect her, I prayed as I rolled down my window and yelled out to her. "I love you no matter what."

In early February 2019, I made the fifth usual Saturday morning three-hour drive. This time, it was cheeseburgers with ketchup only, French fries, and Dunkin donuts coffee. The ride was quiet and slow, passing the Indiana cornfields, the semi-trailers whizzing by. My mind drifted to a time when I didn't know where Marissa was or if she was even alive. I listened to five minutes of inspirational Christian music. I just wasn't in the mood. I turned on classic rock, Free Fallin', and of course, I belted it out as loud as possible.

My mother's intuition kicked into high alert as I went through security. An ominous feeling hit me at once, and I didn't want to go in. I paused, my stomach in a knot. Sitting at the usual folding table, I noticed something was different. She didn't get up to greet me.

Grabbing the bag of cheeseburgers, she looked into my soul and whispered. "You did this to me."

Gasping for air, I recognized "the evil." "What do you mean?" was all I could manage.

"It's your fault I'm here. You and all those people keep raping me." I held my breath,

"No, you're getting better. You're safe here." I whimpered.

"You did this to me." Security came over, and I motioned that I was ok. She gobbled down her lunch, silently watching my every movement. Her eyes were red and bloodshot; her fingernails were long and painted a dark blue. She had marker stains covering the needle scars on her arms where she had obviously been writing on them. She waved her hands, making gestures as if trying to move away objects.

I sat there waiting, frozen. I knew not to challenge this evil persona. Looking through me but at me, Marissa leaned over and whispered, "forever."

She got up from the table. "Here, I'm done."

With the escort and security tagging beside her, I watched the gymnasium door slam. Tears I'd been holding dripped onto the crumpled-up Wendy's bag as I picked up the remnants of this visit. The same look I knew well was on all the faces as I asked to be let out the door. With a nod and, "I'm sorry," the sweet lady led me to the outer security area.

My arms wrapped up tightly to guard against what had just happened, I quickly went to my car. "The evil" voice echoed, and I sat there as the dark clouds came crashing. Fumbling for my keys, I'd dropped on the floorboard. The evil voice seemed to live in the seat where she'd said "forever."

Shivering, I started the engine. It took two hours just sitting there trembling before I could drive. Pulling on my sweater over my shoulders, I made the resolve that it was going to be ok. Marissa was here in this hospital because she was very ill. I had forgotten for a short time she was disabled. There is no cure for this illness, and she will have good days and bad. I was relieved I was the only one who had come to see and hear her.

Pausing to be grateful she was safe and able to get medications. Thankful someone was caring for her twenty-four hours a day.

I pulled into Starbucks for yet another cup of liquid encouragement and because it wasn't safe for me to drive through my tears. For a few minutes, I let myself be sad…I didn't want to make this drive every other weekend. I wanted to stay home and enjoy my family. To relax. I didn't even remember what that was. So many years of living with so much uncertainty had trained me to celebrate the good. Why couldn't I just have a "what do I want to do this weekend?" Fun? What was that? I had a big pity party. Starbucks pity party, table for one…

Inhaling as much air as I could, I let out the world… Stop! My daughter was alive and doing the best she could. I couldn't fix her, but I could be there as much as possible. She wasn't in control of her illness. Be grateful, I reminded myself as I sipped the hot americano. Slowly and deliberately, I pulled out into my world. I thought of the innocent baby boy and loving husband waiting for me at home. There is always something to be grateful for. Something to look forward to. The dark cloud followed me down the road, but I was determined to fight and look for the brightness. I knew I could find it. I would just have to try harder. I felt the "I got you" hand once again.

Sitting in the garage, I gathered my things, and Adam came running to greet me. "I missed you, Momma. Can I have a cookie? Poppy said I have to ask you." It was the simple things one should never take for granted. This sweet little toddler with his golden hair and his, please let me have a cookie, smile. My husband, with his hugs, held me together. A warm embrace that fed my soul. I felt like the luckiest person on the planet in those moments after returning from that dreadful scene. Dogs on my lap sleeping, a toddler with his tablet nuzzled against me, and my good-hearted husband sat in his chair. We settled in to watch Longmire on Netflix.

Deer played by the road on the long stretch to our dream house in the country. I had been to the YMCA to allow Adam social interaction. We had gone to the grocery, where he screamed and threw pods of coffee across an aisle. He knocked down a display of Toll House chocolate chips. You guessed it, he wanted to make cookies. "I want cookies!" He belted at the top of his lungs as he slapped me across the face. Slapping. This was his new thing.

Toddlers are challenging. "Headstrong" and "obsesses" were words I regularly saw on his evaluations. "Has trouble with transitioning." Yeah, I know. When he is playing, he likes to continue playing. He doesn't want to change when he is doing something he enjoys. Well, neither do adults, so I get that. But, he has to learn to behave. Lord, help me.

I was fifty-five, and it'd been a while since I'd dealt with a toddler. I had all girls who were stinkers, but not like Adam. He was determined to get his way, and his smile could melt anyone's heart. And he knew it. He was really good at, "I love you, momma," as he moved his eyes to the cookies I had just said no to. Toddlers are the most expert manipulators. Even the best transportation brokers I knew couldn't come close to the tactics used by these little ones. With the brightest hazel eyes, he would ask, "where are the gummy bears?"

My husband once told him no when I had gone by myself to the grocery. When I returned, I looked at our brand new seventy-inch tv with a massive hole in the middle. "It was his red metal tractor," my husband explained as his eyes wandered to the trash. "I took care of that tractor with my hammer," his eyes filled with anger as Adam just sat on the couch swinging his legs back and forth, without a care in the world.

February wind whipped the car while I drove, watching for the deer, and my mind wandered off. So many things had happened in such a short time that I had to pause to take them all in. My mind would always wander on this stretch. Today was no different, and I tried not to relive the weekend before and the visit with Marissa. Trees sparkled with the icy remnants of the morning's freezing rain. Such beauty in those dangling frozen drops of water with the sun glistening through them. So peaceful with my toddler asleep in his car seat in the back. I let myself relax.

Startled, the phone in the console buzzed and rang. I checked the road and glanced down to see who it was. Unknown number, a feeling came over me. I knew I needed to pick up.

"Hey, mom, I need your address. I'm going to live with you, yeah, ok?" Quickly, I pulled the car off the road. Stunned and overwhelmed to hear my precious middle Marissa's voice.

She was committed to the state hospital? I don't understand. I thought to myself as I contemplated what to say.

"Mom?" Marissa repeated.

When she was committed to the hospital, I thought that was it. She would be able to stay there. Naivety again was not my friend.

"They let me out, and I want to live with you, Mom." She pleaded.

I was devastated. "That's not an option right now," was all I could whimper.

"Why not?" She started crying and said, "I just need you."

I thought of the last hospital visit and glanced in the rearview mirror at my sleeping toddler.

The dark cloud came upon me. "A lot has changed. I love you. Try your dad."

"Mom, you said you'd always have a place for me." Her tears echoed through the phone as it went dead.

"What the hell is going on?" I heard my ex's familiar hostile voice from the past. It was the first time since I got married eleven years earlier that he had called me directly. He left a nasty message on my voicemail the night of my honeymoon.

"I have no idea," was all I could say, and he backed off his hostility.

"What are we going to do?" He said she had come there and knocked on the door, and he didn't want her to stay.

"I have a friend down the street," is all Marissa had said, and he told me she walked away in the freezing rain. He had given her a jacket and something to eat.

"I went and tried to find her," his voice quivered.

"I told her to call me back, and I'd try to figure something out. Do you know if she really has a friend?" Both our lives were shattered by the inability to house her. Both of us tried multiple times. It was so devastating to turn her away. We agreed if we could find her, we'd at least get her a room for the night at the local hotel.

All parents just want the best for their kids, and I was tormented by where my precious middle daughter could be. Angry, I had no warning this could happen. There could have been a plan, a halfway house, or another hospital. Why would they release her to the street again? Why? Where could she be? It was so cold outside. I hoped she'd told the truth about this "friend" that she knew.

Her dad frantically searched his apartment complex. I called and drove around where she had been sited the last time she was homeless. Her sister Elyse looked in her drug world.

I watched my phone while exhaustion crept in. Marissa visited my dreams as a little girl. She hopped up on my lap. "Mommy, read me, Alice." It was her favorite book. Winter wind wrestled the trees by our window.

The slapping of the branches against the glass startled me awake. No, I just want to stay with Marissa. *Please, Lord, let me go back to that joyful dream.* I thought. Adam had his little head on my shoulder. It took me a second to return to reality that my Marissa was grown, schizophrenic, and homeless. I laid and cried endless tears as Adam's comforting locks swept my face.

For two days, there was no word or sighting of Marissa. With the temperature dipping to fourteen degrees with no wind chill, her chance for survival if she was unprotected... I shuddered at the thought. My mind played endless, desperate ideas. Marissa could live in a camper parked behind our house, or maybe we could get a mobile home or maybe rent her one.

Still shocked this could happen, I called and emailed her probation officer. "They released her to the street. I'm so sorry...I didn't know until I got the notice that her probation had been terminated." His voice was full of disgust. All along, he had tried to be helpful. There just wasn't anything he could do.

A doctor at the state hospital found she could comprehend her charges, so they transported her back to the jail. The courts dismissed the charges the next day. They just released my beautiful, schizophrenic, disabled daughter Marissa to the wicked streets. There was no plan. She was just left to her own defenses with nothing. How was she supposed to get her medications? What was prescribed? **No warning!** How could this even be possible? And now. She was missing. They wouldn't put out a missing person since, technically, she wasn't supposed to be anywhere. We just couldn't find her.

On the third day, I was driving around looking for Marissa. In the back seat of my car, I still had the homeless care packets with the blanket, pillow, and water, peanut butter crackers, baby wipes, cereal. My phone startled me as an unknown call registered. I braced myself for the worst.

"Mom, can you take me to the grocery store?" It was the sweetest sound on earth... Marissa's voice was shaky, but I knew it was her.

"I'm so glad you called; I love you so much. I've been so worried. Do you have your medicine? Of course, I'll take you." I rattled off, blubbering and crying. I picked up Elyse to ride along with me. As I drove to my ex's apartment complex, my heart leaped for joy as I saw Marissa by the sidewalk.

"Can you take me to Meijer?" She asked as I hugged her, but no one was home again.

Her huge oversized coat swallowed her body. The smell of stale cigarettes lingered. She was red-faced from the cold. Her pupils were pinpoint and empty.

"Thanks for taking me." She drifted off as we made the ten-minute drive. "Wait here, don't come with me," she commanded as she got out of the car.

She shuffled across the parking lot in the new tennis shoes that I'd gotten her for Christmas. The bright-colored "need coffee" pants, now worn and bare in some spots, could barely be seen from under her dad's winter coat. I saw her making the familiar hand gestures. "Are you sure you don't want help?" I yelled out the window as the freezing air showed my breath.

"No," is all I heard as she waved me off as the sliding doors closed.

Staring at the clock, I noticed the time, 1:33 pm. I had to pick up Adam from my mom's house at about five.

My youngest daughter and I waited and made small talk. "It's so cold. Where are you staying? How have you been?" We talked about Adam and how he's such a stinker. I told her about the metal tractor and our broken tv. We both tried to avoid making words that made sense about what was happening with Marissa.

After what seemed like a million years, I decided I would try to find her. We had scoured both entrances for this long forty-five minutes, so we knew she was still inside. As the freezing air hit me, I saw her at the farthest door, which was not the one she had entered. She looked all around, and I waved my arms around like a person lost in a crowd. Staring all around, she just stood there with her basket, and I ran to her side.

"I got lots of candles. See all the candles." Marissa excitedly announced while she continued her hand gestures following the orbs. She started laughing and said, "Ok," and looked in every direction. I guided her to the car and put in the groceries. "Back to my friends, but you can't help me in." She laughed her schizophrenic laugh and talked to the "voices" on the ride back.

Elyse helped place the candles and groceries on the curb. "Are you sure I can't take these in for you?" Elyse pointed at the pile of snacks and candles.

"No, thanks for coming." She waved, making hand gestures dismissing her, and started talking to the "voices" again. Heavily, the door hinges creaked open, and one by one, she carried her bags of groceries into that dark hallway.

Helplessness and hopelessness crept back in as I pulled back out of the parking lot.

"Where do you want me to drop you?" I asked Elyse. Hugging her tightly, we shared the grief we both felt. We made a "visit with Adam" plan as I got her some burgers and dropped her off at her friend's house.

At my mother's house, Adam came running to greet me. "We made cookies, momma." His tender excitement was such a welcome change to the mood that surrounded me. It was hard to suppress what had happened. I didn't want to be a burden, and I tried not to talk about it. Joyfully, I hugged my sweet little boy.

My mom and dad sitting watching cartoons and drinking coffee were so far from what I had just done. My mind was wandering to, what's next? Just then, my oldest daughter Naomi walked in. I hugged her with glee. Rare and cherished are the days that I got to embrace all three of my biological daughters. One should always be thankful and grateful and hug your kids each time you get the chance. My thoughts rambled at how anyone could ever take their children's presence for granted.

I made sure to look at Adam with his grandparents (or great-grandparents). Naomi had my beautiful granddaughter in her arms. I felt so thankful to have all these blessings. Celebrate the good, I reminded myself as I clung to the words. Keep trying to find the route for my mentally disabled daughter. Pulling out of my mom's house, determination led the way. I would find the answer to where Marissa could live. There had to be someone or somewhere that could help.

The next day it was quiet—no word from Marissa. Adam was sleeping, so I could call the endless list on my notepad. A message from my ex on the special Marissa email popped up.

He wrote: "Apparently, she was staying under the stairwell in that building. The police brought Marissa to my apartment and asked me if I was her father. I agreed to let her stay the night." There were no real friends. Marissa had been sleeping with candles under that stairwell, and someone had turned her in. She had all the blankets curled up in a giant ball and had been hiding underneath. Her laughing and the candles attracted the attention of the neighbor's who lived in the upstairs apartment.

My Ex made a strict list of rules and said he would try again. He made Marissa's appointments and attempted to get her into a few programs. I called all the suggestions from people who said, "there's a gap." She disappeared for three days, once. My Ex found her living in a lean-to on the side of a hill. We both got so jaded from pleading and begging. All the phone numbers we got someone to answer all said, "no, we can't help." It went on and on and on. We tried every angle and kept trying to reach Marissa. She finally disappeared entirely for several weeks. Sleep was a ghost. When I did sleep, she would always visit me— tormenting me with her giggles of joy from her childhood.

"Unknown" registered on my phone again, and I knew that it was the police or a person that found her. "Do you have a daughter named Marissa?" She's here by Randolph street. She's hungry, and she's not making sense. Getting the directions, I didn't know what to do. What if I did find her, then what? I'd give her the packet and a ride to the shelter or a hotel for the night. At least I'd show her I was not abandoning her. I was trying to find a solution that worked for everyone. She was important! She needed her to know how much I loved her and how much I cared.

When I got to the address, Marissa was gone. Driving to the area the lady directed me, I settled my thirty-eight revolver in its tank top holster. This was one of the worst parts of town. The click of the locking car and leaves under my feet seemed like the only sound around. I scoured for signs of her: footprints or food wrappers or blankets or clothing. I tried to imagine being in her shoes. I went block by block; I knocked on doors no one should. I showed her picture to the alley people. Too dark for me to see anything else, I clicked the door unlocked and just sat there.

As I dialed 911, I heard myself say. "My disabled daughter is schizophrenic and out here somewhere. Please keep an eye out for her. Please be careful with her. She is fragile. Be gentle with my precious daughter." *Lord, please let her be ok.* I started the car and glanced all-around before pulling into the street that I knew she had been seen walking down.

Chapter Eighteen

HOPELESS

⟨≈⟩

"Resisting arrest." I saw the summary come across online. I kept hoping she was in jail. At least that was safer than the street, and I could attempt to get her more services since this was a different county with more programs. In the county jail where Marissa previously had been, they don't do "evals" on anyone. There's therapy. If the inmate requests it, of course. But in this county jail, they have "evals" available for inmates like Marissa. That was the gist of what I learned.

In my best, "please, she is disabled" mom's voice, I tried to convince them to send her to the hospital. I was hoping at least they would send her to the local mental facility for her twenty-third visit. At least that would buy me some time to find somewhere for her to live. "There's no evaluator available," I heard as they hung up on me.

Drinking my coffee the following day. I read "ROR" on the online summary. Tears welled up as I reread "ROR." Released on her own recognizance? What? The girl needs a hospital, a doctor, and medical attention. I just don't understand why schizophrenia is not treated as a significant illness all by itself. She is disabled! If this was a brain tumor that made her act this way, she could get real help! Real help!

Angry, I was so angry! For the next two weeks, there was no sign of her. Trying to go on with my life and act normal? Good luck with that. Focusing on the rest of my life, I forced myself to think of all the other people surrounding me. So many blessings. I just wasn't strong enough to push away the thoughts of Marissa wandering around in that harsh world. I couldn't find a solution; I couldn't find her. No one could understand the devastation in my heart. Glancing all around everywhere I went. Thinking every brown-haired woman walking down the street might be her. Driving around for hours in the homeless areas in hopes of spotting her. Misery crept into my soul and stayed.

8:34 am on a Saturday in August 2020. I had just made my second cup of coffee when I heard a Facebook ringer. It was my phone. It was one of Marissa's childhood friends Angie.

"Hey, have you heard from Marissa?" "She was found unresponsive." At this point, I was just waiting for the walls to crash in on me.

As my heart sank to the floor, breathless, I said, "Where? Is she ok?"

Angie explained that "some guy" in Louisville sometimes lets homeless people sleep on his couch. Marissa evidently used his phone the night before and logged into her Facebook, and didn't log herself back out. When he tried to wake her the following day. She wouldn't wake up. After calling 911, he got on her Facebook and tried calling her friends.

"Thank you so much. Do you know if she is ok?"

"No, I just know she was rushed to U of L Hospital" Angie's voice was shaking.

With the POA in hand, I stumbled through the turning door at the ER of U of L Hospital. "Can I help you?" After rambling through the endless story, they pointed me to a tiny waiting area. Three horrifying hours I sat in that tiny room. I memorized every voice and shuffle of the staff hustling to get everything done. When my patience was done, I walked to the reception greeter.

"My daughter? Please help me find out what is going on".

The Chaplain is the one that approached me. "I don't know what's going on," is the first thing he said, so he must have seen the sheer terror in my face. He listened like a Chaplain would, and I was relieved to not be alone. Rules at the hospital forbid anyone else to come in. With the promise he would try to get someone to update me, he walked back down the hall.

Another miserable half an hour later, the ER doctor came out. "Can you just tell me if she is alive?!" I contained my scream.

"I'm so sorry." At that moment, he realized no one had told me anything. "Yes, she is alive, but she isn't responding to us." I breathed for the first time. "We're waiting for more test results, but so far, we don't have more information."

Catatonia, a stage of schizophrenia. As briefly as possible, I gave Marissa's life journey synopsis over the last few years. "Maybe her mind is broken?" The doctor was kind enough to spend more than five minutes listening. I could tell he was genuinely perplexed by her condition.

"She's disabled with schizophrenia." I tried to make him understand the severity of her illness—anyone who knows how the disability process works knows that proving a schizophrenia diagnosis is extremely difficult. There has to be concrete, long-term, ongoing, can't fake it, proof. And after one submits the evidence, Social Security assigns their own psychiatrist and subjects the patient to yet another three-hour intensive evaluation. I hate those that try to fake it. I want them to spend one day in my daughter's tormented mind. I want them to walk in my shoes as a mother of a schizophrenic. That would be the best punishment. I caught my mind wandering off to keep from falling apart.

"Can I see her?" I asked as I forced myself to stay calm. I wrote, "she's alive," and hit send to the others waiting to hear.

184

"She's awake but not responding," he repeated. "Yes, you can see her." He motioned to the receptionist to lead me to room three.

Through the crack in the door, I could see her foot hanging out from under the white hospital sheet. Dark blue polish scraped partially off. Scars from previous needles were evident to someone who knew they were there. I wanted to break down. Pausing as the bricks crashed the wall I had built for an emotional guard. I eased open the door and stepped into the darkness. Blank, there was no emotion in the room except mine.

Beep, beep, beep, the machine registered each heartbeat. Nurses took her vitals. "Are you, mom?" I could only nod. When open, her eyes, once blue and sparkling, were vacant. Just a blank stare and then back to slumber. Her arms were covered in large bruises. They were awkwardly turned outward and jerked a couple of times. Scars from needles and a brown recluse spider were openly visible. Mostly, Marissa wore long sleeves, so I hadn't seen her scars lately, and I found myself staring.

How could this be happening to my beautiful daughter? She was a dancer, a theatrical performer, a magical gift of beauty to all who knew her. I glanced up at her face, those little girl freckles now covered with scrapes and bruises and filth.

"We'll clean her up soon," the nurse noticed as I took in the gravity of her face. "She's been mostly sleeping since she's been here." The nurse must have thought I needed to hear that.

Lord, please help my sweet little girl. Laying my hand on her hand, I prayed. I struggled as I always did for words to ask the Lord. *Thanks for my blessings, and you know the rest,* was my normal as drifting off after going through my list of concerns led to more beer than sleep.

After a few hours of watching her, I texted. "She is mostly sleeping, still not responding." to the group text I had created for those concerned about Marissa. My husband and Naomi, who had been waiting outside, went back to their lives. I stayed. Knowing that if she woke up, the evil might erupt, I tried to make the staff aware. "She thinks she can kill people and bring them back when she isn't medicated."

I couldn't leave her side while I had this rare chance to sit next to her. For the next two days, she was in and out of consciousness. Warning the doctors over and over that she was off medication. They should not let her be alone with anyone. They should be cautious with needles and forks. Be aware. She is not on her medication and does not have control of her severe mental illness. When I heard myself say all this out loud, the dark cloud ascended once more... I didn't want to be there. I didn't want to say those things. I wanted my daughter back! Tear after tear didn't ease the tragic reality that I admitted. I didn't want her to wake up. I wanted to be able to care for her in this place. To sit next to her. To feed her.

The hospital assigned a volunteer to sit in her room at my insistence. On the third night, she made hand gestures but couldn't speak. "Do you know your name?" Marissa's left finger came up and waved back and forth as if to say no. "Do you recognize her?" The psychiatrist pointed to me. Marissa's right finger came up and down to signal she knew me. How could that be when her eyes were void of light or dark. I put my hand on her arm. Nothing, I felt emptiness. Dark, lonely, emptiness.

Please put her on the psychiatric floor, I urged the doctors. She was coming back to consciousness. Please move her before she becomes aware of her surroundings... I begged the staff with all my motherly persistence. As I fed her chocolate pudding and reveled in this extraordinary moment, knowing any second she would awake to her harsh reality. I allowed myself to dream this event somehow would cure her like the movie with the girl that fell out of a tree. Miracles are possible.

I prayed aloud. "Lord, take away her illness and let her mind be free."

On the fourth day, she was talking. "Do you know her name?" The psychiatrist asked, pointing to me. She recited my full name as if she was practicing. My heart sank as I realized she was going to remember. I didn't want that for her. I wanted her to remember her childhood full of joyful dreams and puppies

187

and kittens and all things good in the world. I tried to protect her from her mind that rehearsed an unending nightmare. "Do you know what year it is?" the doctor asked. Marissa shook her head. "Do you know how old you are?" Again she shook her head. "Do you know your birthday? Again, No… she couldn't remember. She was having trouble with simple words and phrases. Maybe there was a chance for her to start over. I let myself be hopeful.

Sitting in the uncomfortable hospital side chair the next day, I let my mind drift. I tried once again to frame a home for Marissa. Who else could I call that may be able to help? Maybe being in a different state would be the hope she needed. Kentucky has much better resources, I had once been told. As soon as she was admitted, I reached out to social services. They started a file for her. I pulled my purse onto my lap and rifled around, looking for the lady's card. They still had Marissa on the medical ward, and when the nurse came in, I asked when they were moving her to the 'fourth' floor. I looked him straight in the eye, intentionally not saying which floor that was. "Oh, the Psych floor?" It was hard to prevent myself from punching him as he whizzed out. I looked over to see if Marissa was listening. She was…

"I'm thirsty, really thirsty. I need water now." She arrogantly insisted. The volunteer leaped up and walked out to get her water. (which she wasn't supposed to do) Abruptly,

Marissa's voice hushed. "Leave. I don't want you here. Leave now." The evil voice took me off guard, and the chilling depth of despair rushed in. The volunteer hurried in with the water and glanced up at me. My face must have painted the picture of terror, or maybe she felt the presence. The eyes of the devil looked straight into my soul. "Why are you here?" Marissa glared at me.

Shocked at this voice, the volunteer offered. "This is your momma, honey. She's been here for several days."

Against the evil's leave order, I stood by her side for over an hour.

"Leave, you need to leave now. I know my rights, and I don't want you here!" Marissa's evil voice pierced the air as security rushed in.

As they escorted me out of my precious daughter's room, I stopped at the nurse's station. "Please, please move her to the psych floor, Please!" I begged.

Leave? How could I leave? I sat on the curb, staring at the street. This was the bad part of town. A block away was where all the riots and murders went down. Definitely not a safe place to tremble. My husband was on his way, so I moved inside the ER area. Exhaustion took its turn with me, and I slept all the way home. I prayed again with my little boy sleeping next to me in my comfortable bed. Please Lord, help my daughter, save her mind from this torment, and I drifted off. Fight, you must fight the darkness. That is not her. It's the illness that plagues her. I knew this, but my dreams screamed at me. Don't give up. Keep trying to find a way. You have to fix it.

The following day I took Adam to the YMCA once more. I went a different route; I didn't want to travel the road where she had called me. I called the hospital to check on Marissa. "Let me get someone to talk with you." I waited so long I had to hang up to go in, and once I checked Adam into the nursery, I called again. "Oh, no one picked up? Let me get someone to talk with you," said the same operator. Ten minutes, fifteen minutes, nothing. I called again and got the same operator again. This time I simply wanted voicemail so I could leave a message.

"Please let me know an update on my daughter," and I rattled off her name and birthday and what room she was in. I barely remember the thirty minutes of watching HGTV on the screen on the elliptical machine. My sweet boy was in rare form as he ran under the play fort and hid and threw toys at me and slapped me across the face… again.

"No, I don't want to go." Adam hurled his plastic truck at me.

"I'm glad you had fun. Want to come back tomorrow?" I asked him. Nodding as I picked him up, kicking and screaming and flailing around. I wrestled him to the car. We weren't out of the parking lot when he was fast asleep. Pulling his limp body from the car seat in the garage, the phone rang. As quickly as possible, I lay him on the couch.

"Is this Marissa's mom?" A person from the hospital asked.

"Yes," I stammered, frozen at the gravity of what she may say.

"I wanted to call you myself," she said, and she told me who she was. She was there when they did Marissa's psych interview. She checked herself out of the hospital ADA this morning. She started screaming about knowing her rights and that we couldn't hold her against her will. "I'm so sorry to tell you— We did everything we could. I'm so sorry."

Gasping for air, I paused at the horror. My precious daughter had walked into the most dangerous part of town with nothing, no clothes, no food, no money, no shoes, nothing. The doctors hadn't had enough awake time to assess her for medications. There were no tools to guard against the schizophrenic demons that wished to rule her body and mind.

"No, please no," is all I could manage as I dropped the phone. No one could have consoled me. Death's breath came down my neck, and I couldn't stop the tears. Amid my wailing, my sweet little boy had awakened from his nap. His sweet soothing voice was a beautiful contrast to the defeated reality of those moments.

"Momma, why are you crying?" He rubbed his sleepy eyes as I hugged him too tightly.

"It's Auntie Marissa. She left the safe place." Genuine child's eyes reflected his confusion.

"Is she going to be ok?"

I swallowed my tears. "We can ask God to protect her." I soothed him. With his unique look of sheer toddler determination, he cupped his little fingers together as we knelt next to the bed.

"Don't be sad, Momma. I love you." His hug conquered the darkness that hung in the air.

Chapter Nineteen

JUST KEEP GOING

Marissa had vanished. While Adam was at school, I scoured her previously sighted places. Holstering my gun, I walked into the bushes where the homeless hung out. Care packages kept them from seeing me as a threat. I knew what the homeless wanted most was for someone to care. I brought emergency blankets, towels, baby wipes, granola bars, baby food pouches, and cereal. I questioned and showed her picture to anyone that would listen. She was simply gone.

For two weeks, I lived with the torment of my thoughts of where she could have gone. Her birthday was spent looking for her once again. She had simply vanished. I tracked what-ifs and maybe's, running every scenario. There had been riots in Louisville at the time she was gone. I frantically searched the crowd of homeless on the news for a glimpse of what may be her. My number had become a regular incoming call at all the local hospitals and jails. When "my Ex" showed up as a text message, I quickly grabbed the phone.

I read: Marissa called me around nine am this morning. She was in old Louisville and asked me for help. I left work right away and found her. She agreed to go to the shelter in Jeffersonville, Hope Mission. We met with the new owner and successfully got her into the Path program today. She was given some new clothes and food. Then they took her to a quarantined hotel where she is now. She will have her own room with a shower and bed. A balcony where she can smoke. They will bring her 3 meals a day to her room. She will get tested in the morning for Covid-19. She will have to stay in that hotel for 3-5 days or until she tests negative. After that, she will be taken back to the shelter and begin the program by going to Life Growth for meds and therapy. As long as she stays there, they will help her get into housing, take her to and from Court, and Life Growth. Marissa looked healthy but exhausted. She was not showing many signs of her illness and was very happy when I left and seemed willing to do whatever they asked. She can't receive calls or visitors till she is out of the hotel. I pray that this will be the answer we all have been waiting for.

It was the best text I'd ever gotten. I breathed deeper than I had in years. Relief was such a welcome emotion as I believed Marissa would finally be ok. Maybe she was cured of this horrifying illness somehow. Maybe the hospital stay had somehow brought on a new beginning, a new chapter of Marissa vs. the world. Maybe I could have my daughter back. My prayers had been answered. Happy tears flowed while I watched the slumber move in and out of my innocent toddler. Trying to stay focused on the positive, I fought the vision of our last encounter, and the demonic voice that I knew wasn't her. I wanted so badly to believe she was somehow miraculously cured.

I would love to bring her Tiramisu and Qdoba for her birthday. I texted back. I tried to explain that last visit to the hospital and how I needed to step back from personal contact with her. After the previous graphic episode, I found the words to make him realize I had to sell my car. It's haunting words repeating with every grocery run. Not comfortable putting a toddler in his car seat with that demonic presence still hovering. I was so grateful to my Ex. I never stopped praying he would be happy. Thankful for his wonderful fiancé, who stood by his side. I was so relieved he was living his best life. Grateful that time helped both of us heal. Working through this maze of Marissa's illness brought us to speaking terms. At the very least, it has been good for our other two children to see that we could work together.

I'm having trouble with my right brain. I asked to be taken to the hospital for a few days to get my medicine and to stabilize. The text from my Ex quoted Marissa. It always amazed me the strength it must have taken for her to fight these demons. The courage to be able to say out loud what was happening. He text: She said they will take her over to Clark Hospital soon.

Another huge thing for her, she hated hospitals. I told her that she was doing the right thing, and I was incredibly proud of her. She started to cry and said thank you, Dad. Then I heard someone say, are you ready to go and she said bye.

Tears ran down my face as I read his words to me. Clark hospital has access to real help, long-term help. I was hopeful she could be put on track for permanent placement. A home where she would have daily activities and structure, and quality of life. Somewhere safe! Monitored, but with privileges. That would have been the best arrangement for someone that really needs to maintain daily medications. Lord, please protect her and guide her. I prayed.

'They said she had started laughing a lot lately.' The mission person explained to my ex. The director said she was doing great. They had dinner, and she had just taken her meds. She had met with her caseworker and was scheduled to go to Life Growth the next day. She went outside after she ate and vanished. She left all her stuff.

Reading the text aloud, I realized my precious daughter Marissa had walked out again into the darkness. Once again, my little girl was homeless. Defeated by the emptiness that comes with the journeys of the mentally ill. I inhaled the world as to be able to exhale this news. I lay on my bed, unable to comprehend what I could possibly do. I was so tired from the strain this illness brought. Numb from the constant disappointments. Enraged at her for not staying where she was safe. Afraid of what may happen next.

Another agonizing two weeks went by. With Adam off to school, I called and called and called every hospital, police station, people who had sighted her, mental health facility, and shelter. Drove around with my gun and packages for the homeless. Nothing. Again there was no sign of her. I thought to myself. What would I do if I did find her? I couldn't allow her in my car. Not after the last haunting encounter both in my car and at the hospital. I resolved that I would try to take her to the local shelter again or the hospital or give her a blanket and some clothes and warm food. At least she would know that I cared and was there for her. Maybe she would agree to go to the hospital. I lied to myself. I needed to sleep at night. Being responsible for a little man, I couldn't just take something to help me sleep.

Going on with my days, I made my usual yearly trip to Dale Hollow campground for my anniversary. It was a family and friends four-day adventure of fishing and fun. Adam loved it because they would do the trick-or-treating and everyone decorated their campsites. The year before had been a complete blast. Celebrating my husband and me and the years we'd been together.

This year felt so different. How could I focus on having a good time with a toddler when my thoughts trailed to my missing, homeless daughter? Misery behind my fake smiles and forcing myself to join the campfire dinners. Drinking more than my usual two beers in hopes that would somehow ease the reality. My youngest Elyse had come along, and I welcomed the help with the seemingly nonstop, relentless toddler. I welcomed time with Elyse that was joyful.

Startled out of the memorizing campfire, tears welled up in my sister's eyes as she excitedly held out the phone. Gabe, tell her what you just said. "I saw Marissa at Chick Fil A; she looked good." He excitedly announced.

Relief mixed with anger as I sat down to let my thoughts settle. At least I knew she was alive. He went on to say she was walking down the street, and he happened to pass her. Marissa was very close to where her father used to live. She probably went there because it was familiar, and she was a big fan of Chick Fil A. Numbness took my tears of joy. Although it was great to have someone see her alive, her illness was in control. The demons couldn't be trusted, but I allowed myself to pause and try to find hope.

My loving husband's hugs eased that world as I watched the scene of my family and friends celebrating our wedding around the campfire that night. A new breeze wrapped hope and grabbed the sparks that whisk away into the night. The family stories all unfolded. Laughter and joy were found in this magical wilderness campfire. Sleeping toddler on my youngest lap smells of cider and marshmallows, peace for the moment.

My mind drifted back to that last car ride home from the mental hospital. Stop! The song says peace for the moment. Exhausted from constant emotions, I slept through the night for the first time in what seemed like years.

"Incoming call" Elyse's ringtone interrupted my morning coffee. I gave her "the look" as she wandered off to have her private conversation. After a few minutes of watching her arms talk, her brow told of concern. Returning to the campsite, her voice intensified.

"Mom, it was the police. They called about Marissa." I froze as I checked my phone and saw five missed calls.

Marissa had wandered back and forth on the same street, asking random strangers for money and food. It was a street we all knew well. A place we all shopped regularly. Target, Qdoba, Chick Fil A, the grocery store, the gas station, and a couple of strip malls with restaurants. All on this slight stretch of road. She was behind Feeders Supply, the officer told Elyse as she tried to explain that we were all on a family trip. Elyse wrestled with the words to explain Marissa's illness and told them to look up her name in the public records. Again her phone rang, and it was another random stranger.

"Do you have a sister named Marissa?" They asked her.

This was Marissa's code for "I'm close to the edge." She would have random strangers dial all the numbers she could remember. Approaching anyone and everyone with the story that she couldn't find her family. She would tell people she was lost. She would give them made-up names. She would cry on a bench by McDonald's, begging for money or for them to call someone. Desperately, her mind was crying out for help.

Dave was a persistent stranger. Seeing no reason why this young woman would be living on a bench in front of Tire Discounters, he questioned my Elyse. The naivety of strangers always made me question my actions or lack thereof. Was I doing all that I could? Is there nothing else? Couldn't I just pick her up and hug her tightly and let her live with us? My heart agonized with every scenario. That evil voice loomed and hovered, visiting my dreams.

Glancing down at the curls barely visible from under my little boy's favorite spiderman blankie. I knew the answers. Without medication, my precious middle daughter Marissa could not defend herself. Her eyes were not her own. But the beaconing of my soul's persistence kept me running every option. Calling every lead, exploring every angle.

Dave's military training showed. "I just don't understand," he insisted. He had brought her food and blankets, and a pillow. He had asked if she wanted him to rent her a hotel room. The kindness of strangers like Dave had kept my daughter safe for these long stretches of homelessness. They would never fully understand the sheer gratitude I had for them.

"I'm on my anniversary trip." Dave got my number from Elyse and updated me on Marissa. He had a radio show about law and wanted to work with the state and local police. Again, I called Adult Protective Services for help. Hoping they should be able to do something about a "vulnerable adult." I kept repeating and assured Dave that I was doing what I could.

Brisk air and campfire, deep blue sky, we walked the dog down the campground path. The leaves were golden melodies of the majesty of fall. Breathe, in and out…relax. Marissa was lying somewhere on that street. She is just walking around; anything could happen to her at any moment. My mind just wouldn't shut off my fears. Trying again to find words for yet another stranger had triggered flashbacks of the many times I had failed Marissa.

Packing up the anniversary trip, I froze at the gravity of her situation. It's something that happens to people who have lost children. Overwhelming grief and sadness take over, and there's just frigid emptiness—crippling mother's guilt for not having been able to find a solution. I knew the scripture about worry. My soul was not open to this ability to let it go. I clung to God's gentle hand.

I forced myself to push her reality to my mind's balcony. I forced myself to stop packing up the campsite and walk to the playground with Adam and Elyse. Hand in hand, we all giggled as Adam yelled, "swing me." Elyse and I launched him into the air as the waves of leaves crackled in the crisp breeze. That dark cloud was my constant companion, but I fought. I held tightly to these miraculous moments. Reminding myself that the good is worth my attention. Rejoicing in the ability to share this spectacular spitfire of a boy with his mommy. The pure joy that came from watching them love each other. *We are all worthy,* I thought. Hope was found here in these moments. In the good.

After we turned to the campsite, we all helped pack up and enjoyed the last few moments around the fire before it was extinguished. Elyse held Adam and hummed softly to him. I prayed that she would continue to improve; Adam needed his mommy to be a good role model. The rattle of the dishes and soft rain brought comfort on the three-hour winding road home. Watching these two miracles together gave me new hope for Marissa. I gained a new resolve to keep persistently searching for a new path.

Chapter Twenty

TRESPASSING

A dult protective services are supposed to help "vulnerable adults." After another twenty-minute conversation with the area coordinator, she actually said. "Well, Marissa hasn't hurt anyone yet."

"Why isn't my disabled adult daughter covered under 'vulnerable adult'?"

"We don't do that," was her answer once again. "We mostly protect the elderly."

"Ok, if she were ninety, you'd do it?"

No answer. At least the coordinator spent this time on the phone with me. They did send an off-duty officer to assess her. He didn't look where I told him she was. But, technically, he said he went to the area. Adult protective services only take people who have guardians back to their homes. Or they investigate abuse cases. There's a huge need for them. But they don't really help vulnerable adults with mental illness.

"Well, in Indiana, we leave that to the family. You could become her guardian." Was repeatedly their solution.

I had met with a guardianship attorney. The answer to who would be responsible for all her actions was "the guardian."

"Could I become her guardian so that I could sign her over to the mental hospital?" I hoped.

"No, there's no guarantee they would take her." The attorney said they probably wouldn't since she had a guardian in charge of her. It was so sad. I would have been able to do it if the demon drug world was not involved. If I became her guardian and she goes back to drugs… I was unwilling to do that. I would not put my family in that situation. Guardianship was not the answer. I know Adult Protective Services wanted to help Marissa. The sad reality is they didn't know how.

Go over her head, I was told by anyone that would listen. I left a voicemail voicing my complete disbelief that no one at adult protective services could seem to do anything to help my daughter. I assumed it would not be returned. Surprised by the Indianapolis area code registering on my phone, I answered.

"Is this Mrs. Stacy?" A stern lady with a deep voice barked. Armed with a long list of agencies to help, the Indiana Adult protective services director personally called me back.

I wish I had a recording of this conversation for all to hear. The state director's stern, stoic voice got softer with each of my answers.

"I've already called them." "I've already tried that." "She has been to that facility twenty-five times." "She's been in that program and wouldn't comply." "They told me she needs a waiver from Medicaid she doesn't qualify for."

After twenty things were marked off her list, she was silent for a few seconds. Her voice trembled as she finally muttered. "I'm so sorry, Mrs. Stacy. I was so prepared to show you all the programs that could help. It seems you've already tried everything on my list."

"There's a gap when they only have a mental illness," I repeated to her what I'd been told by everyone else that genuinely wanted to help.

When Dave called, he said. "Marissa told her name was Jerico There and something about the line. She wasn't making any sense." He'd lost track of her and was worried. She was usually by Chick Fil A about this time. I again urged the police to look out for her or take her to the hospital. One of the officers knew Marissa from her endless days at the county jail. Her sister Naomi got six missed calls from a State trooper. A plan was put to motion with a collaborative effort of that state trooper, the kind local officer, the Feeders Supply personnel, my oldest daughter, and several strangers.

They approached the manager of Feeders Supply. Marissa had been sleeping between their dumpster and the building. Knowing they had been sympathetic to my little girl, they asked the manager to fill out a no trespassing order. Explaining that if Marissa violated it, she would be picked up and taken to jail. At least she would be safer there. With the order in place, the manager watched eagerly for her to return. Once securely in her "bunker of cardboard," Feeders Supply personnel called the number from the card left by the local officer. A sympathetic judge issued a warrant. My sweet precious middle child Marissa was placed safely into custody.

"She's been arrested," Naomi said. My heart sank. Another resisting, another assault, horrible scenarios ran through my mind. "Trespassing," and I exhaled all my air at once.

This was good news, not great because she would probably soon be re-released. I sprang into action! This was my chance again to get her the real help she needed. I resent the letter to the Judge with the added, "she was found unresponsive," verbiage. I pleaded to have a new evaluation done. At least if she were ordered to the state hospital, I would have more time to make some kind of plan for her living arrangement. I reached out for help from anyone that would take the time to hear her story.

At the urging of a few strangers, I emailed the local news. The Judge took mercy and remembered Marissa. She set her bail high and postponed her hearing for forty-five days. It was all out, I will find housing no matter what! Determination of my toddler set in. I was not going to let this opportunity slip by. I could not live with her being re-released to the street.

The clouds became darker with each, "she doesn't qualify." After two weeks, I had zero ideas left. Tears came one by one, dripping on the notebook with line after line marked out with a red pen. Help me find it, Lord. I prayed as I watched my little boy slumber next to me.

Remembering Marissa in scene after scene of horror, I gave up. I gave in to the reality that there was **no one**— No one but **me**. An ocean of despair plunged me deep to the bottom once again. Lying on my bed drowning little by little. Gasping for a small glimmer of an idea that was possible. With my eyes closed, I thought back to my backyard oasis pool. The bottom I had reached in those hopeless moments.

As my thoughts circled like the seagulls waiting for a crumb, I was suddenly jolted by the hand that grabbed me and said, "I got you." Bracing myself, tears wouldn't stop; I was so afraid. I wasn't worthy or qualified. How was I supposed to make this miracle happen? Intentionally, I picked up the notebook and ripped out the tear-soaked pages one by one. When I came to the first page that was dry, I started a new list. The hand of God could find any route.

Without thinking, I wrote. "Buy a house for her to live in." How was I going to do that? My thoughts crashed like waves one upon the other, each more intense. A hurricane of emotions started to settle into a glorious peace. Scouring the internet in my area, I scrolled through listing after listing. The market was very tight. Everyone seemed to be looking for other ways of investing. Looking back, it was incredible that I had more money than usual in the bank at this exact moment.

When the virus hit and business stopped, I urged my husband to sell our big house and purchase a small place in town. Having hated living in the country, I broke the news during my sobbing on a Friday evening that living so far from my family was literally killing me. Already having a dark cloud following me only added to the isolation I felt way out on those ten acres.

At this time, I had no idea how this timing would come into play. It's true love when a person puts their heart and soul into a dream home then walks away purely for their spouse's health. Pure love. Although he was angry for a few days. Ok, a few weeks. My husband's only stipulation was that we needed to buy the house in town first.

Risky as it was, I pulled out our retirement money to cover the cost of the tiny home we could afford. Once we moved into town, we listed our country home. It took several months, but we closed on the big house in September. We were supposed to put the money back into retirement or another investment. Still, it was sitting in our account at the exact time I felt that hand of God.

"I want to buy a house where Marissa can live." I couldn't think of a better way than the direct approach once again. Sitting at the kitchen counter, my husband looked me straight in the eyes. He had already held me together through so much heartache and endless, relentless nights with no end.

"Do it," was his immediate response, just like that.

"Toni, my daughter gets out of jail on Dec 16th; I need a house by then." I surprised my realtor friend. She had handled our little house in town deal. I gave her the list I had made off Zillow. It was already the middle of November. A former funeral home was rough, but I could make it work. Desperation threw logic out the window. It was a maze of sold signs and contract pending.

When Toni said, "I know a deal that just fell through for the second time in a row." I jumped at the chance to see the home. The area was ok, and the house was solid. Old but charming. It needed work, but I could handle it. I didn't have time for perfection or niceness. Safe. I needed a secure environment. The HVAC was newer, and the roof didn't leak. With Toni as my warrior, we made the cash offer that was quickly accepted.

Two weeks later, I had the keys!

Rip out carpet, paint wood floors, luxury vinyl in master. My list was made. Alone in that house, I ripped room after room of filthy carpeting. Cutting it into manageable size pieces, I hurled them onto the curb. Dust clouds poured out of the windows. When it came to installing the luxury vinyl, I hit a roadblock. For three hours, I struggled to lay just one row. I just couldn't figure out what I was doing wrong. I had laid flooring before, but this just wasn't working. I read the directions over and over.

In desperation, I called my husband for advice. I had been determined to do all the work myself. It was unfair to ask him to help with this extra work. He had so much on his plate.

An hour later, I heard his van out front. Nonchalantly, he strolled in with his tool belt, saw, and two crowbars. Tears dripped onto the handle as I watched him tear apart what I'd just spend half a day laying. Angry tears that I needed his help and happy tears that he had come. Plank by plank, side by side, we applied each piece. He said, "it's just tricky flooring," attempting to make me feel better.

The deadline was fast approaching for when Marissa would be released. I had to have everything ready. The notebook list had new red lines marking the things I had gotten done. YouTube was my friend when it came to the old wooden floors. After researching the options, I decided to paint them with a special paint that didn't require sanding.

Artwork from Facebook marketplace and Goodwill, carpet runners from the special clearance, a table I made from an old shutter, it was all coming together. I found coffee cups at an auction and made a cute holder. My grandmother's old sewing machine table made a good coffee station. My husband installed a digital lock on the door. My Ex and I would have access codes to share in the care of our daughter.

Gathering my thoughts, I waited for her call. Sally, the counselor at the jail, had answered my emails and voicemails. She was doing her best to convey any information to Marissa she could. Tell Marissa the rules. Was the next thing on the list.

"Mom, yeah, uh, can you put money on my account? I, uh, need an e-cig." Her words broke up as we tried to understand each other.

"Do you have a plan where you are going to live when you get out?" I didn't want to assume she hadn't made other plans.

"No, can you put money on my account, uh, please, mom?" Click, schizophrenic laughter, and the phone went dead.

I wrote her a letter. "If you will go straight from the jail to the hospital, comply with treatment, and agree to the contract, I have a home for you."

I didn't lie to myself about the chances of this plan working. Scenario after scenario constantly ran through my mind. Marissa was going to have to comply. When she called the next night, I told her the same thing I had written.

"Thank you, mom, I, I love you, yeah," schizophrenic laughter and again click.

I called the jail the next day to find out what medications she was taking.

"Nothing," the clerk rudely answered.

What do you mean, this is an unstable, disabled schizophrenic. *You denied Marissa medication?* I thought. God's timing here was perfectly aligned. Turns out Marissa had been caught hoarding her prescription for a few days at a time and then taking them all at once. This is strictly prohibited and warrants a restriction on all medications. This meant that she would be completely clean when she was set to be released. It's not something I wanted for her. Still, it is harder to start a baseline when you go into a hospital setting if you have to wean off medication first.

Picking out my clothes, I kept thinking. "Where are my lucky pants, my blue shirt, my comfortable shoes?" I couldn't find anything. Yelling at Adam to find his blanket for daycare, I tripped over his favorite spiderman toy, whacking my knee on the side of the table. "Sh*t!"

"Momma, that's a bad word." He looked at me with eyes wide in surprise.

At least it wasn't the F-bomb, I told myself. Breathing in my frustration. Momma sees if Auntie Marissa gets to go to the hospital today."

He wrapped his tiny fingers together in prayer. "It'll be ok, momma." His little eyes sparkled up at me while he hugged and kissed my knee to make it feel better. I scooped him up and gave him a huge thank you hug. Finally, I threw on my "nice" jeans and my "go-to" black shirt. What did one wear to court these days? I didn't really care. I just wanted luck and to be as comfortable as possible.

Tapping on the steering wheel, I caught every light. It seemed to take a million years to drop Adam off and get to the courthouse. I drove around twice and finally parked a block away. Sitting in my car trembling, I Inhaled, exhaled, inhaled, exhaled. I looked around at my old Yukon. Even though it wasn't new, it was my sanctuary. Out loud, I whispered. "Ok, I can do this." I was about to break my vow to never again allow unmedicated Marissa in my car. My stomach was rumbling, and I grabbed Adam's cereal stash. I wasn't about to listen to my rumbling stomach on top of the fidgeting wave of my crossed leg. Get out of the car! My subconscious took over, and I opened the door to my fears.

Earlier that week, I had called the clerk's office multiple times. I made my argument over and over. Someone finally gave me the advice to come early the day of the hearing and present the Power Of Attorney. The sympathetic mother of an addict promised she would make sure the public defender received them but couldn't guarantee he would speak to me.

Appealing to his nature, I used my best pleading mom's voice. "She's disabled. I'm trying to help her not be homeless." Adding. "What if that was your daughter?" I've tried this tactic before at one of her many doctor's visits. One of them actually said to me, "I can't see my daughter being like that."

While restraining from slapping her I fired back, "I'm so glad you are immune from humankind."

I prayed for that lady as I burned her card in the firepit. I remembered the naive days when I believed I could control what happened in my children's lives. When the wrath comes down, she will be so unprepared. My thoughts drifted. Blaming the parent for a child's addiction or mental illness was a naive person's way of thinking.

"Mrs. Stacy? "The public defender called from his office door. Marissa, lost in outsized orange, was already seated at his desk. He looked me straight in the eye with the "I see now" nod. It was clear he had attempted to speak with Marissa.

I started my rehearsed monolog. "I bought a house for her to live in, but she has to agree to go straight to the hospital."

Broken, lost, and confused, my child sat trembling, her feet uncontrollably oscillating back and forth, trying to dig out of this existence.

"Marissa, is this what you want?" He asked her as he tried to gain her focus.

Nodding her answer, she started to cry. Not now, I thought as my tears remained paused.

"Sign here," and he attempted to explain to her the case and courtroom normalities.

"Thank you for taking the time." I nodded to him. I hugged Marissa's shell, which wasn't supposed to be allowed. I felt her painful emptiness and confusion as the awaiting officer led her away. It was another hour waiting until the courtroom opened and all the families and accused filed in.

"All rise." A hundred shattered lives creaked the benches at once. Marissa's head jerked slightly from side to side with the familiar twitching of the non-medicated mind. From behind, her hair looked darker, and I felt her blankness. Chills of the past made me shrug uneasily. My hands grew cold, so I tucked them under my legs as I sat.

The rare inmates with attorneys presented their cases, followed by the indigent inmates with public defenders. Hopeless, endless cases of the addicted and afflicted past in front of the Judge. As I heard her name, I had to refrain from standing.

"Marissa?" the public defender nodded at the inmate next to her, who lightly nudged her. Seeming not to understand, she stood and shuffled in front of the same Judge that signed her Lack of Capacity decision.

215

"Marissa, do you understand your plea?" She nodded sideways, mumbling yes.

"Where do you plan to live?" The public defender addressed the Judge, " her mother has secured housing if Marissa agrees to go straight to Lifetime."

"Is her mother present?" I raised my hand like a grade-schooler. The Judge nodded with a hint of a smile. I only guessed that she was glad to see a glimmer of hope in this endless row of misery.

"Her mother has arranged an appointment with intake at 1 pm." Marissa's public defender added.

"Who is going to transport her?" the Judge inquired.

"I will," my voice split the air as the Judge looked me in the eye. I was hoping she didn't see the terror I was hiding.

"Marissa, do you agree to be transported by your mother straight to Lifetime?" The Judge asked her.

"Uh, yeah, ok, my, my mom," Marissa turned and looked at me.

"Do you understand she will only take you to the hospital?" The Judge stressed.

"Yeah, yeah, ok, I go, ok," Marissa answered, bobbing her head side to side and twitching, biting her lip, her schizophrenic nerves in control, her eyes darting around.

"The court accepts the agreement." The gavel thud brought a thousand echoes of evil. God's got this! I blocked the darkness.

I choked down the last of my cold vending machine coffee. Once decided, I had asked the clerk how long it should be before she was released.

"It varies." She said, but I knew that answer. Marissa was well known at the county jail. My constant calling hadn't gone unnoticed, which struck me as strange. Marissa wasn't the only mentally ill person there. I know they were sick of my constant insistence that she should be in the hospital.

They agreed, under the circumstances, to do everything possible to help her be discharged quickly with the agreement signed by the Judge. I was allowed to come to the lobby and have her released only to me. Not to the street. Fidgeting and cross-legged, my foot waving back and forth. I sat waiting. Sally, the jail counselor, buzzed out the door. She felt like a friend from the many conversations we'd had over the years.

"Marissa's getting out," I announced.

"That's wonderful! Marissa was so relieved when I told her you had a place she could live," Sally assured me.

Understanding the gravity of my nerves, she stood there with me as the door alarm buzzed. A few genuinely remarkable people worked in these jails, and Sally was one of them. Being led by an officer, my precious middle daughter Marissa emerged.

217

The buzzing seemed louder as the door slammed, and the officer disappeared.

Comforted by Sally still by my side. We both greeted Marissa. "Stay on the right track Marissa, do what your mother says, ok?" She attempted to catch her gaze, but Marissa's head was flailing around.

"Thank you for doing what you could." I shook Sally's hand as she walked into the large hall to the courthouse.

Throwing the fuzzy blanket with bright colored, "you got this" over her shoulder, Marissa fell into me. My little girl in my arms brought me tears of joy. No matter the circumstances, we lingered, mother and daughter in a warm embrace. For so long, Marissa didn't want anyone to come near her. But at this moment, she allowed me to feel her vulnerability. I lingered a little too long... She pulled back and looked down at her tennis shoes, two sizes too big. They squeaked the floor as we exited the safe harbor of the jail lobby.

"Where are the shoes I got you for Christmas?" I nervously asked.

"Uh, yeah, this mean girl stole 'em." Marissa rambled. Later she explained that this girl tormented her when she was homeless and had taken all her stuff. "Can we get cigarettes? I really want cigarettes, please just, please, I need cigarettes, coffee, and a cheeseburger. Can I get a cheeseburger and cigarettes? I really need cigarettes, yeah?"

"We can get a pack on the way, but you have to stay by my side. We'll go right there." I pointed to the gas station visible from the sidewalk.

"You'll let me smoke in the car?" She mumbled.

"This one time."

I pulled up and got her out of the truck. The clerk rang us up, one cheeseburger with ketchup, a pack of Camel Turkish gold, a coke zero, a Nestle Crunch, and water. She had a lighter and loose change in her personal belongings that had been laminated to a piece of cardboard. I struggled to open it without any sharp objects as she stood over me, twitching her head side to side and stammering.

I motioned her to sit back in the truck. "Put on your seat belt and eat your burger." I finally got the lighter free, and the loose change scattered with my thoughts. "Here." I handed her the lighter. She took a larger puff than a person should be able to inhale and coughed out into my face.

Waving it out, she said. "Sorry, mom, I'm sorry, uh, thank you, uh, sorry."

One cigarette after another kept time as we slowly made our way to the mental hospital. Jumping out of the car was a voice Marissa had often heard, so I knew not to drive on the highway.

Washing down my nerves and the Nestle Crunch with the last bit of water. I gathered my nerves. "Let's go." I motioned to

Marissa. Her hands trembled, and she bobbed her head side to side, glancing at her shoes. "You can do this, Marissa." I tried to reassure her as I saw fear take over. "You want one more cigarette?" Slowly as she could, she took draws and trembled, blowing her smoke out of the corner of her mouth in one little trail. "Your room will be waiting, but you have to stay until they say you are ready to be discharged."

Solidifying my resolve, I pulled out my phone and showed her the bright-colored walls of her bedroom and the blue pictures. "I bought you a new pillow too," I told her as I slowly pulled her packed bag out of the trunk. She agonizingly wrestled out of the seat. "It's going to be ok. I am so very proud of you." I started to cry but managed. "You are the bravest person I know."

My thoughts drifted to the many times I'd stared at this sidewalk. How much torture she had gone through fighting with her mind while she courageously walked next to me. She leaned away as I reached for her hand. I wanted to skip with her as we'd done in so many parking lots in the past.

"May I help you?" The receptionist asked.

"This is Marissa; we had an intake appointment at 1 pm." The door alarm blared, their keys clanked, the waiting, and the same interview started. All so familiar, all so horribly dark. The same beige color walls, this time with the imprint of a fist from a previous session.

"Do you feel you're going to harm yourself?" This is a question they are required to ask. It's a trigger question along with "do you feel hopeless."

Immediately answering in her jittery, schizophrenic mumble, angrily insistent, "No, I love myself."

Tears came abruptly rolling and dripping while I tried not to panic. There was no guarantee they would admit her. I hadn't considered this! In all the planning and execution, there was never a scenario where the hospital didn't admit her.

The interview door crashed behind me. Sitting and waiting seemed to be what the world of mental health held. For two hours, I watched my little girl's mind torment her as she twitched and mumbled in an unending battle. All the while forcing my own thoughts from wandering to the darkness that encircled just waiting for an entrance. The door creaked open, startling us both, and slammed shut.

"Sorry that it took so long." The interviewer looked at her feet as she sat. "The doctor was with a patient, and I couldn't interrupt."

I don't think I breathed for the next few minutes as she read all the papers and went over the programs.

"We're going to admit her." she finally said.

Visibly shaken, I sighed way too loud. Marissa's head was bobbing side to side with her legs crossed and bouncing, stuttering and mumbling. She had no expression. The blankness chilled the air, and I felt my hands move toward hers. I hugged her but, again, she wasn't there.

For the twenty-sixth time, the alarm split the air as the door slammed behind me.

For the twenty-sixth time, I sat balling in my car at the reality that played out in this place. How could I believe this time would be different when she'd been here so many times before? I went over the events that had perfectly formed to allow me to sit here in my truck. God's magical symphony of a thousand little motifs. Grief overtook me at the thought of leaving my daughter once again. I knew she could walk out of this safe place if the evil overtook her. The fear kept circling my mind like a vulture.

Another hour later, God's hands held me together as I started the engine. My truck made its way to the little house that was Marissa's. On her porch, I paused and prayed. God, please protect her. Once more, I checked to make sure there were no sharp objects, all was ready, and all the doors were secure.

From the truck, I called Naomi, and she put me on speaker. "She's in the hospital." She and my husband exhaled their relief. Once home, I pulled the sleeping boy from my side of the bed, and I slipped under the flannel sheet. Hugging Adam tightly, I prayed again. *Thank you, Lord, for the peace of this moment.*

A week into treatment, They started Marissa on a new medication. A new shot. Marissa's dad had visited, and things were progressing well. Armed with more photos and pictures of outfits. Marissa and I went over the things she wanted to eat. I asked her to spend time making a list of places she might want to go. What about a bicycle or walking in the park? How about an easel and painting supplies? If this actually worked out, what next? It was as if I was trying not to trip in the dark. Blind to what lay ahead. Unable to trust that she could get well enough to care for herself, I analyzed every scenario. Praying as I steadied my thoughts toward positive outcomes.

"Where's your ID?" I asked Marissa. When a person becomes unstable, the situation worsens if they don't have a proper ID. "Where is your license?" I repeated.

"Uh, I, by a tree? I think." She answered.

Scouring through hospital paperwork one by one. I knew a copy of her license was in one of those files. I believed it was the file from when she came to live with us. Or it was in the hundreds of pages I'd sent to Social Security. All I needed was a copy so I had the number and could request a duplicate be sent to her PO Box. Covered in file after file, my bed looked like a puzzle. I did my best to keep everything organized.

Adam, playing spiderman shooting webs in the sky, flew through the air and landed directly in the center of the bed. Papers scattered and flew halfway to the ceiling.

"Stop!" I yelled at him for being a typical three-year-old. "Stop jumping on Auntie Marissa's papers. Go out now."

Picking up one paper at a time, I saw him out of the corner of my eye.

"Sorry, momma, Spiderman is sorry too." His eyes welled up with big crocodile tears.

"It's ok sweet boy. Momma is sorry for yelling. Let's put all these back on the bed and go get a cookie."

"Momma, can we make more cookies?" Adam's lip puckered.

"If you give me a kiss," I answered, and he leaped in my arms from the top of the couch, nearly knocking me over.

"I love you, Momma." His innocent hazel eyes glanced at my soul.

"Only one more cookie, then we have to eat an apple." I looked at him with a smile.

"With peanut butter?" He grinned.

"Yes, with peanut butter."

"Ok, momma, deal." He held out his little hand to shake mine.

Staring at the piles of paperwork scattered, I noticed a folder that read: Marissa's first hospital stay 2013. That's it. Spiderman Adam had saved the day. Flipping the pages one by one, trying not to notice the words, the patient talked to the dead people trying to get her to solve their problems. On the twenty-second page of intake papers, there it was! The copy of her license from 2012. Carefully ripping it out from the staple, I held it like a baby. This piece of paper held the key to getting Marissa's medical benefits reinstated. Knowing her disabled status, the hospital allowed some time for me to get that ball rolling. I made the BMV account online and requested the duplicate with the number in hand. Thank you, Lord.

"Your duplicate license has been sent." Little things piled up one after the other, hurdles in the endless hoops of Social Security. At the same time, I was grateful; I was exhausted by the nonsensical questionnaires. "She has already been found disabled. I'm trying to help her get back on her feet." I said to the staff at the Social Security Administration. I told them, adding, "she is mentally disabled; she can't fill out the papers herself." Seriously? She's in the mental hospital now.

I talked with a handful of beneficial, sympathetic men and women at Social Security over the years. But the things they were required to ask got entirely ridiculous. I realized once again that the countless people who continued to take benefits by faking made things so difficult for those of us mothers of truly mentally disabled adult children. I prayed not to hate them. Day after day, with her release coming quickly, and the shot's three thousand dollar a month price tag, I kept diligently calling.

Chapter Twenty-One

HOME

Going through my garage, I found some old CDs from the good days when Marissa's dad and I were first together. Dust flew in my face as I pulled the old case from the past. Find a hobby that gives her joy. It was always on my list. Tap dancing didn't work out too well. I had already marked off journals, gel pens, and art supplies. With her Christmas money from my parents, I bought her a small tv and set it up in her room. I hoped she would want to watch Netflix if the "voices" were calm. Music, maybe she would enjoy music.

Carefully, I pulled each cd from its graveyard of years gone by. Happy memories flooded this box of youthful existence. I wanted that feeling for Marissa. I prayed for the fun this music brought her dad and me to somehow manifest through these melodies. It was Dec 29, 2020. She had been scheduled to be released on the 26th, but Marissa's doctor added a new medicine at the last minute and wanted to make sure she managed it well. I carefully wrapped the unique gift of happy memories.

Twinkling lights sparkled atop the small Christmas tree I put up in her living room. No visitors, no exception. The posted sign in the mental hospital lobby broke my dream of spending time with Marissa on Christmas. I settled for "Merry Christmas" through a phone line.

"We'll celebrate when you get home," I told her and sang, ``We Wish You A Merry Christmas.

"Oh, thank you, mom." She said they had a small party and turkey dinner. They'd brought in donated gifts for each patient to open. She spent Christmas in a hospital for the second year in a row.

This slapped me in the face while I stacked presents under her tree. Her sweet little voice in front of the mirror with her plaid leotard "Look, mommy, I grew into this body," when she was four. The dance competitions, the trip to Hawaii when she whined about it being cold, those mesmerizing deep blue eyes. I could still hear her Lily St. Regis impression from Annie. That was her favorite character from all the plays she has been cast in. She nailed it perfectly after practicing and recording herself all night. Tears dripped onto the bright color Nightmare Before Christmas wrapping paper. Stop crying. Stop. At that moment, I wasn't really sure if these were tears of joy that she was coming home or tears of sorrow for my lost little girl.

"Venti white mocha," the drive-thru was busy, but it was worth being armed with Marissa's favorite Starbucks distraction. The truck drove itself to the familiar mental hospital parking lot as my mind checked lists. Red lines on the notepad, one after the other, I went through scenarios. If I could just think of all the bad things that could happen, maybe I could prevent them. I lied to myself.

"I'm so excited." Marissa's voice was a sweet melody compared to the "uh, yeah" I heard in court. She kept saying, "I'm so excited," over and over while we went over her discharge on the phone. Sitting in the parking lot, I sipped slowly on my Americano. God's got this. I kept telling myself, but the door to my truck wouldn't open. Tapping on the steering wheel, I flipped on the radio. You're a Heartbreaker, Dreammaker. No, how about Christian music? Oh, No, you never let go, through the calm and through the storms. "Not now, Lord," I said out loud as I switched the radio off.

I had chosen the same black shirt and "good" jeans I wore to court. I figured I needed as much luck as I could get. I paused at the reality that Marissa would soon be seated next to me. I longed for her to be normal, but the acceptance was made. I hoped she would be able to simply walk down the street, or skip in the parking lot, or go to the mall. Hoping for her sake, she would be rid of the constant torment of the "voices," hallucinations, and people raping her every night. Pulling the lid off my coffee, I breathed in the last of the warmth. Inhale, exhale, inhale, exhale. You can do this, Get out of the truck! Slipping slightly on the ice, I caught myself just in time. Slowly and steadily, I deliberately watched every step—one at a time.

Christmas is a mental person's nightmare. The saddest, the loneliness, the isolation are all magnified a thousand percent during the holidays. Standing in the lobby, all the seats filled, I shuffled my legs back and forth. This was going to take forever.

The presents were under Marissa's tree, the banner was hung, no sharp objects were in my truck or in her house. Check, check, check. Tick, tick, tick, I watched the mindless show on the lobby tv. Eyes jerked all around. Twitching drug addicts fought with their loved ones. Arm crossed punks pulled their hoods over their lost childhoods. The air in these places is either too hot or too cold. Always. Never comfortable, Never. The ever-present buzz of the door and clanging keys, sometimes welcoming discharged patients, sometimes to allow in a new intake.

"Mrs. Stacy?" I heard the buzz and my name.

"Hi, mom." For a second, we paused and just looked at each other.

"You look wonderful!" Joyful tears streamed down my face. Hugging her, feeling her. Swallowing hard, I regained my composure. "You ready?"

Marissa handed me her bag. "I'm excited," she repeated.

229

"I got you," I said as I held out my hand; we walked out into the cold. Slowly, we navigated the icy sidewalk one step at a time.

"Your sister is coming to meet us."

"I'm excited. Can we get cigarettes?"

"I already got you a pack and a lighter," as I opened the console.

"Thank you so much, thank you, thank you."

"You can't smoke in my car." I gently reminded her. Two long drags later, she blew out the smoke from the corner of her mouth.

"Let's go," smiling as she leaped into the seat. Smiling, my little girl was smiling! The tears welled again as I hadn't seen her genuine smile since the visit to the State hospital. Stop, not now. I have to drive. I told myself as I pulled out of the parking lot.

Together for the first time, we made our way on the icy roads to her house. Navigating the potholes one by one. No way to avoid these inescapable holes. No way to go around. No way to find a different route. We navigated side to side through them. Slowly, cautiously, deliberately. It was bumpy. But manageable. I watched as Marissa's head bobbed furiously side to side, her eyes wide like she was riding a roller coaster.

"Those are some big potholes," she giggled. Her eyes lit up from the distraction of the tense scene she'd been in so long.

The anxiety of years of struggle was released, bobbing and weaving through these potholes.

"You're home; this is it!" I shouted my excitement. She was speechless. Her blue eyes stared at the wonderment of her very own place to live. The "blessed to be home" mat didn't go unnoticed as she took in every detail. She plopped into her rocking chair on the porch and swayed back and forth.

"This is so awesome!" She was giddy.

"Those are roses. I bet they're going to be beautiful in the Spring." I pointed to the row of bushes in front of her porch. "I think that is a redbud tree." We went over the landscaping. "This is the digital lock I told you about." We went over the operation, and I made her promise to always keep it locked. Naomi pulled up just in time to watch Marissa walk into her house for the first time. We did the "thumb trumpets," and she opened the door. She marveled at the Christmas tree and all the presents.

Marissa opened Naomi's gift first. A sweater and scarf. She threw it on and modeled it for us, practicing her runway moves. Tearing open the paper and throwing it over her head, she gazed at the box of CDs. "These are the CDs your dad and I listened to when we were first together." Someone had gotten her a Walkman-type player, and she threw in a disc.

"I love this." Burnin' Down, The House was done, and Marissa was getting tired.

Naomi said her goodbyes. Tightly, I hugged her and thanked her for being there. I was so proud of Naomi's pure good-heartedness. My beautiful, talented, first-born child. I prayed as she walked off the porch. *Lord, please protect her.*

Marissa kept repeating, "this is so awesome," and "I'm so excited." I went over the contract and made sure she understood the rules emphasizing that all this went away if she did any illegal drugs. Stressing it was binding on both of us. She could live in this house, and I would act in the capacity of her guardian, as long as she abided by the rules. With drinks in hand, we signed the document. "Cheers," our glasses clinked, and we sipped our Coke Zero. When she lay down in her bed for the first time, she snuggled into the pure cotton comforter. I saw her again as a little girl wanting me to bundle her up like a burrito. I knew it was time to go.

"We need to get your medicine for tonight. Do you want to come or rest here?" I asked.

"No, I want to stay right here." She patted the soft blanket and looked up at me with a twinkle in her eye I hadn't seen since she was eight.

"What do you mean you don't have it?" The clerk at the pharmacy explained that they were out of the medicine Marissa needed. "Can you call around?" I hugged Marissa and assured her I'd be back with the medicine. I showed her how to work the tv. The smile never left her face.

Hugging her again, "Enjoy your home." I said as I closed her door.

"The store on tenth street has it. They're open until nine." The clerk at the pharmacy said,

"It's eight forty-five pm. Will the clerk wait?" I bolted down the alley—no time to avoid potholes right now. I had to make it, or she wouldn't have her required pm medicine.

Eight fifty-nine pm, I pulled into the drive-through. I had called and made sure they waited. "Thank you, my daughter has to take this tonight." He gave me the "I get it" nod.

Waking her with the water and meds, Marissa said, "thanks, mom, I'm gonna sleep. I love you."

"I'm so proud of you. I'll be back in the morning with your AM meds." Sitting in the car, I couldn't stop the tears. My precious middle daughter was sleeping in her bed. Back at home, I listened to the comforting snores of my husband and little boy. I prayed. *Thank you, Lord, and you know the rest.* Exhaustion grabbed me, and slumber was my friend.

Day after day became an endless drone of medications and appointments. Marissa had so many adjustments to make. She'd been homeless or in jail for two and a half years. One night she called the police because she thought she'd been stabbed. Tactile hallucinations still plagued her, and her wounds felt real. She was transported by ambulance to the hospital but refused treatment.

At 12:02 am, my phone rang. "Mom, can you pick me up from the hospital?"

"Of course, I'll get there as fast as I can."

Back at her house, I looked all around. She was convinced that she had killed Santa Claus.

"It's ok, mom, I'm ok now. I'm sorry, I'm sorry, I, I, just." Marissa always had the same sad-eyed, horribly embarrassed look when coming back from an episode. She remembered them but couldn't control them.

"One day at a time." I kissed her forehead. "I love you no matter what. You're going to have good days and not so good; just take one day at a time. Celebrate the good."

Four months is the sweet spot when the medicine takes its full effect. Monthly doctor visits, monthly shots. Marissa's dad and I shared the chore of watching her swallow daily am and pm medicines. Day after day, we updated each other on food and watched her take her pills and all things Marissa.

"How would you like to go to the beach?" I asked Marissa. To have her in a state that she was well enough to travel was magnificent. Maybe someday, all my daughters will be well enough to tell their own stories. Maybe Marissa could realize her dream to publish the poems she'd spent writing every day. The book Naomi and Marissa had worked on over the years. I let myself dream.

"Yes, the beach!" Marissa said excitedly. If I ever got the chance, it had been my goal to take my daughters on a beach vacation. No one would have thought I'd be able to do this rare event. With one daughter barely ninety pounds, living in her car, hooked on fentanyl, the other lost to schizophrenia and homeless on the harsh streets. Naomi couldn't make the trip since she was expecting a baby and was too close to her delivery date. My youngest daughter Elyse was on board.

"I can't wait!" Elyse said.

Marissa's meds had to be planned out. She had this window of five days a month when her medicines worked the best. I orchestrated our three-day beach vacation around these wonderful five days after receiving her monthly shot. I allowed myself to get excited.

At the airport, we all locked arms and skipped through the terminal. Waiting at the gate, Elyse sat with her legs swaying back and forth, biting her nails while she ordered a huge beer at nine in the morning. Elyse hadn't flown since our fabulous family vacation to Hawaii when she was eight. Rolling my eyes, I watched as she set her beer on the ground only to move her foot slightly, sending cold Bud Light for the carpet to drink.

Yes, people were staring at us. I had gotten black matching-themed tee shirts. Mine said, "It's ok to be a little different," with a lady bathroom sign on one side and a rainbow unicorn on the other. Elyse's shirt said, "support squad," in the silver support color of schizophrenia. Marissa said, "schizophrenia warrior" and the Wonder Woman symbol. With Marissa's matted blue hair, carrying her blue stained pillow, laughing her nervous schizophrenic laugh, we were quite the crew. Now we had spilled beer in a huge circle, bringing out every other hidden smell.

Inhale, exhale, I grabbed my purse. I handed Elyse a twenty. "Just go get another one, and I'll help you drink it."

We sat waiting for our flight, sharing a twenty-two-ounce beer. *Maybe I'm the crazy one?* I thought to myself. The reality of spending three days in a condo with these two sent my crossed leg bouncing. I was never so glad to have an on-time departure. Marissa hugged her blue hair-dye stained pillow with her blue-stained hands visible as if it protected her from the world. Elyse was biting her nails and twitching, but not a withdrawal symptom, and I took a moment to be so thankful for that.

The plane ride, the car rental, the forty-five-minute drive. We made it! Throwing our bags on the floor, we walked to the boardwalk and onto the sandy paradise of the beach, hand in hand. Something about the salt air and the waves crashing. God's majesty revealed. Thank you for this moment. I paused as I watched my schizophrenic daughter play with her recovering drug-addict sister. At the same time, the waves weaved in a miraculous crescendo. I was so thankful for this spectacular time with these amazing women.

With sand still in our shoes from skipping on the beach that morning, we made our way back from the airport. Marissa's eyes opened to the possibilities that once seemed unreachable. The lady that stared at the street signs had been moved to a different housing project. It must have been precisely six o'clock. It was a fire hydrant that now held her captive as she waited for the secrets to her world. Marissa knew her and watched her intently. I believed she knew what that hydrant would say. We both hugged Elyse as we dropped her off at a friend's house. We turned a few more corners and pulled into the road to Marissa's house. A journey we both knew well.

The smell of oil and hot tar ripped the air. The "children playing" sign kept me ever aware as we slowly crept closer to the familiar potholes. The gray was a sharp contrast to the newly paved section of the road. Speeding up as I saw them, those potholes were now black pavement; I intentionally drove right through the middle. It was still bumpy, my truck bounced, and our heads bobbed slightly uncomfortably. But at this moment, there was no need to go a different route.

One day at a time, one pothole at a time, God filled in every hole. He helped us find a way. He watched over my daughters and pulled me from the bottom. He gave me strengthening light in the darkness. Although Marissa still needed daily care, God cleared the path with an army of angels;

my first-born child, my cherished youngest, my steadfast loving husband, and the father of my children.

God's got this. He took the reins of our souls and guided us along this road of despair and grief. Thanks to Him, me and my daughters, side by side, tapped and skipped to the peace in this moment.

The end was only the beginning.

Acknowledgement

Special thanks to my daughter Marissa (not her real name). I know the non-mentally ill person we all knew, would like trying to save others from the things you have endured. I love you so much.

Thanks to my husband for putting up with my constant doubt. Shout out to my biological daughters without whose encouragement this book would never have been completed. Thanks to my friends and family for doing their best to be there for us.

My daughter would not be alive if not for the special care and attention of the many health care workers, police officers, support staff, and well-meaning strangers.

Edited by: PaigeLawton216
Beta reader jenniferconr549
Cover design by: king of_designer
Formatted by: @accuracy4sure_publishing
Thank you We Love Memoir for their hilarious and motivational Facebook group.

God's got this and held me up through this entire journey. May he bless all who read this with whatever they need to keep fighting and keep believing.

My sincere thanks for reading,
J Mark Stacy

Author Bio

J Mark Stacy spent thirty years as a transportation broker, not a career she chose. Attending Indiana University Southeast, she studied nursing and business. She has written numerous stories and poetry. Her works in progress include a children's book and a fictional psychological love triangle thriller. After blending families with her husband of thirteen years, she has eight children and seven grandchildren. Daily, she continues to care for her schizophrenic daughter (As of January 2022), still searching for hope in the midst of this debilitating disease.